I Am

Walk in Divine Confidence, Supernatural Boldness, While Being Free From Rejection, And Emotional Wounds.

The Power Is Found In The I Am

Samaria M Colbert

Scripture quotations are from the Holy Bible. The New King
James Version: Containing the Old and New Testaments.
Nashville TN: Thomas Nelson, 1985. The Message Bible:
Eugene H. Peterson, 2002. New American Standard Bible

Table Of Contents:

Part 1: The Source

Part II: Destiny Killers

Part III: The Antidote

Preface

The anointing flows through confidence. It is so important that Christians not only walk in confidence but divine confidence that only comes from God Himself. There is a difference between just being confident in yourself and being confident in God. We will talk about this further in the chapters to come, but it is important to know that when we talk about confidence we are not talking about the secular or worldly definition of confidence. We are talking about a God-confidence, which comes as a result of having a relationship with Him. When you have divine confidence, the supernatural power of God can be released in your life. You'll see God move in exponential ways that you wouldn't have seen otherwise. God confidence gives supernatural ability, boldness and divine acceleration in every area of your life. Unfortunately when you lack God confidence there will be a delay and in some cases denial of your destiny from manifesting. Imagine praying, believing and having faith for something, then God finally gives it to you, but you can't receive the gift, you can't see it, you can't touch it all because of one thing, and that is lack of confidence. I am convinced that many Christians do not see their ministries come forth, many are not seeing their destinies fulfilled all because of lack of God-confidence. Yes, being confident may appear to be a menial thing but what you will learn by reading this book is a major kingdom principle. We are breaking strongholds off the body of Christ through this information. One statement that I will repeatedly say throughout this book and as a forewarning I will sound like a broken record "The anointing flows through your confidence." And to the contrary, 'the flow of the anointing is stopped, and prevented from flowing when confidence is not present." Confidence is not the anointing. There are many people who are confident but not anointed. Confidence is the main ingredient for the anointing to manifest. It is like baking a cake; you need certain ingredients in place before you put it in the oven to bake into a delicious cake. That is how it is with confidence it is the ingredient needed for the anointing to be present.

Let us go on this journey together; your life will be changed as you read this book. It is indeed heaven sent.

Part 1: The Source

Chapter 1

A Counselor's Confession

Psalm 118:8 (KJV)

8 It is better to trust in the Lord than to put confidence in man.

Before we get started, I have a confession to make. As a therapist and a writer, I have spent many years counseling, writing, and learning how to build up others. The truth is the reason why I can write this book and many others like this with such conviction is that I know my stuff. If there is one thing that I struggled with for many years, that was lack of confidence. It started as a child and grew as I grew. I never had any confidence in myself. A few months ago, I had a conference on Divine Confidence, and I told the participants my truth. I told them how I struggled with low confidence for many years. I am set free, delivered and whole now of course, but it hasn't come without a process. I didn't get confident overnight. In fact, I honestly don't remember being happy as a child. I didn't enjoy most of my twenties. I have spent more of my life self-loathing, self-defeated and insecure than I care to say. When the process of learning to love myself came, the transformation of life is so amazing people literarily don't recognize me. I know what it is like to feel as if you are not worthy, like you're not good enough, to listen to the voice of the enemy telling you, you don't belong. I have been suicidal because I felt as though I didn't deserve to live. Oh, but God. Today I am a woman who is deeply in love with God. I love myself flaws and all. I realized confidence was not found in perfection. Confidence was not found in being the right size, the right color, the right shape, having the right degree or the right man. Confidence is found in God. Had it not been for God I don't know where I would be. My point is not to brag by any means. I have accomplished more in my life than I ever anticipated all because of God's grace, mercy, and unmerited favor. Nevertheless, none of it would have happened until I finally stopped believing the lies of the enemy and started seeing myself the way God's sees me. I write from a place of true conviction, not from the expert trying to get information to you, but as a person who has been there. I know, I understand, my misery has now become a part of my ministry. I am grateful for the finished work of Christ. Without Him, true transformation would have never taken place. First, let's start with some interesting principles about confidence and what happens when a person is not confident.

Whenever a person is fearful on a regular basis, they lack confidence.

Whenever a person cannot effectively communicate their needs, wants and desires they lack confidence.

You cannot walk in God's authority, power and presence without confidence. The anointing flows through confidence. Lack of confidence stops the move of God from flowing in your life.

What stops people from writing their book or accomplishing their goal has nothing to do with lack of resources, lack of time, but rather lack of confidence.

Ability is not confidence, but when you are confident you know your ability.

What stops people from pursuing their dreams is not lack of faith rather lack of confidence.

What stops people from speaking up even when they have something important to say that could change lives is not because they can't speak or don't know what to say rather because they lack confidence.

If when you get around someone who walk in any level of authority, you shy away, you lack confidence.

If you become intimidated by successful people, you lack confidence.

When you are overly concerned about people's perception of you, and you worry that people won't like you, you lack self-confidence and struggle with the spirit of rejection.

When an individual never speaks up for themselves, allows other people to treat them negatively, that individual lacks confidence.

When an individual is easily offended, passive, very defensive and doesn't have a teachable spirit because they can't handle critique, these individual lacks confidence.

Lack of confidence and the spirit of rejection go hand and hand.

Lack of confidence is a barrier to your relationship with God. You can't grow in God with lack of confidence. God will tell you who He has created, you to be and you will reject His words no matter how positive and affirming they are because you lack confidence.

Low confidence is like cancer it will impacts every area of your life.

Imagine with me wanting something that is your heart's desire. You pray and pray, quote scriptures, read the word, fast about it. Year after year, you wait for the promises of God. Maybe you are praying for a spouse; maybe you are praying for financial stability. Maybe you are praying for your ministry to take off. Year after year, you wait. Year one goes by; you wait, year two goes by you wait. Year, after year, after year, you wait. Sometimes you wait encouraged, sometimes you wait discouraged, sometimes you are content, but you know what God has promised you.

Finally, there it is, your ministry is about to take flight. You are now at the place of manifestation. Maybe you meet the spouse you have been praying for, for all those years. They are everything on your list and then some. Maybe the dream promotion is finally there; you will be the CEO of a major fortune 500 company. There you are minutes, second, days away from something you prepared for your whole life. Then something happens, and you stop dead in your tracks. You turn back around and never move forward to destiny.

What happened you may ask? Good question.

Fear happened. A little voice in your head, what we know as thoughts. The thoughts say, "you can't do that, this is too much, you're going to fail, that is not for you, you don't belong here, that person doesn't belong to you, look at them and look at you. They are perfect; you are a mess." On and on the thoughts go. You believe your thoughts and turn around never to be seen again.

The sad truth is you can be right on the brink of the greatest breakthrough in your life and fear, lack of confidence can stop you dead in your tracks if you allow. It may sound odd for some, but it can and does happen. I can prove it. Turn with me in your Bible to Numbers 14. Before we read, let me set up the preface for you. The people of Israel had finally gotten within feet of the promise land. This is after going through hundreds of years of slavery, being released, walking through the red sea on dry land. You heard of the miracles. This is after seeing great signs, wonders and miracles. Food fell from heaven, their shoes never wore out, there was a huge cloud following them to show them the way. Clearly, they had the hand of God on them. They survived great battles and won by God's hand. You would think by the time they got close to the promise their confidence would be secured in God.

They get there, the place they had longed to be at and prepared for years. Regardless of the toil, struggle and stress through it all, there was one thing that they kept on their minds, they going to the promised land.

They are right there; they can see the promise. They can't just walk up in the promise; they need to scope it out first, see what it looks like, consider if they are going to have any opposition. Moses has a bright idea; he wants to send spies out to take a look at the land and then come back to report all that they see. This is very wise of Moses, so he does just that. This is where we will begin reading out text. We will be reading this from The Living Bible Version and the New King James Version. Let's start with Number 13.

Numbers 13:16-21 (NKJV)

16 These are the names of the men whom Moses sent to spy out the land. And Moses called Hoshea[a] the son of Nun, Joshua.

17 Then Moses sent them to spy out the land of Canaan, and said to them, "Go up this way into the South, and go up to the mountains,

18 and see what the land is like: whether the people who dwell in it are strong or weak, few or many;

19 whether the land they dwell in is good or bad; whether the cities they inhabit are like camps or strongholds;

20 whether the land is rich or poor; and whether there are forests there or not. Be of good courage. And bring some of the fruit of the land." Now the time was the season of the first ripe grapes.

21 So they went up and spied out the land from the Wilderness of Zin as far as Rehob, near the entrance of Hamath.

Numbers 13:26-33Living Bible (TLB)

26 They made their report to Moses, Aaron, and all the people of Israel in the wilderness of Paran at Kadesh, and they showed the fruit they had brought with them.

27 This was their report: "We arrived in the land you sent us to see, and it is indeed a magnificent country—a land 'flowing with milk and honey.' Here is some fruit we have brought as proof.

28 But the people living there are powerful, and their cities are fortified and very large; and what's more, we saw Anakim giants there!

29 The Amalekites live in the south, while in the hill country there are the Hittites, Jebusites, and Amorites; down along the coast of the Mediterranean Sea and in the Jordan River Valley are the Canaanites."

30 But Caleb reassured the people as they stood before Moses. "Let us go up at once and possess it," he said, "for we are well able to conquer it!"

31 "Not against people as strong as they are!" the other spies said. "They would crush us!"

32 So the majority report of the spies was negative: "The land is full of warriors, the people are powerfully built,

33 and we saw some of the Anakim there, descendants of the ancient race of giants. We felt like grasshoppers before them, they were so tall!"

Are you seeing what happened here? In the King James Version it reads,

Numbers 13:33 King James Version (KJV)

33 And there we saw the giants, the sons of Anak, which come of the giants: and we were in our own sight as grasshoppers, and so we were in their sight

Notice all they did was spy out the land. They didn't have an argument with the Anakim people. There was no indication that the Anakim people even saw them. The Anakim people didn't say they were grasshoppers, the people of Israel assumed that the Anakim people saw them as grasshoppers.

My point is what was really stopping them from going into the promise was not the enemy, it was their perception of how them saw themselves. Maybe they were weaker than the enemy. Maybe the enemy could defeat them. Still, they had God on their side and a promise from Him. This is why confidence is not found in our ability, it is found in God. When they cried out, they said, "we can't do this." They also were doubting that God would get them the promise land. They lacked trust in God. When a Christian has low or no confidence they really don't trust God.

Now let's go to Number 14. We have to look at how low confidence spreads. We also have to consider God's response. As a warning it was not pretty. God was not empathic towards their wrong perception, in fact He took great offense to them. He decided that all those who doubted were not fit to get to the promise. Come let's read the text together.

Numbers 14:1-11 Living Bible (TLB)

14 Then all the people began weeping aloud, and they carried on all night.

2 Their voices rose in a great chorus of complaint against Moses and Aaron.

"We wish we had died in Egypt," they wailed, "or even here in the wilderness,

3 rather than be taken into this country ahead of us. Jehovah will kill us there, and our wives and little ones will become slaves. Let's get out of here and return to Egypt!"

4 The idea swept the camp. "Let's elect a leader to take us back to Egypt!" they shouted.

5 Then Moses and Aaron fell face downward on the ground before the people of Israel.

6 Two of the spies, Joshua (the son of Nun), and Caleb (the son of Jephunneh), ripped their clothing

7 and said to all the people, "It is a wonderful country ahead,

8 and the Lord loves us. He will bring us safely into the land and give it to us. It is very fertile, a land 'flowing with milk and honey'!

9 Oh, do not rebel against the Lord, and do not fear the people of the land. For they are but bread for us to eat! The Lord is with us and he has removed his protection from them! Don't be afraid of them!"

10-11 But the only response of the people was to talk of stoning them. Then the glory of the Lord appeared, and the Lord said to Moses, "How long will these people despise me? Will they never believe me, even after all the miracles I have done among them?

After the spies came back, they gave a bad report. But, Joshua and Caleb were different, they were confident that God who brought them through the wilderness would indeed get them to the promise.

Cleary the people of Israel were not interested in hearing what they had to say. Look at God's response.

Numbers 14:26-30Living Bible (TLB)

26-27 Then the Lord said to Moses and to Aaron, "How long will this wicked nation complain about me? For I have heard all that they have been saying.

28 Tell them, 'The Lord vows to do to you what you feared:

29 You will all die here in this wilderness! Not a single one of you twenty years old and older, who has complained against me,

30 shall enter the Promised Land. Only Caleb (son of Jephunneh) and Joshua (son of Nun) are permitted to enter it.

What is your promise? What have you been praying to God about? What would your response be if when you finally see it, it is so vast, so huge, that it intimidates you? My point is you can be right at the brink of the greatest breakthrough of your life and lack of confidence in God can stop you dead in your tracks, and stop you from entering into

the thing your heart has spent years preparing, praying, struggling and fighting for. By the way the people of Israel who didn't respond well didn't make it to the thing that God had promised them.

Numbers 14:37-38Living Bible (TLB)

36-38 Then the ten spies who had incited the rebellion against Jehovah by striking fear into the hearts of the people were struck dead before the Lord. Of all the spies, only Joshua and Caleb remained alive.

Just because you have a promise from God doesn't mean you will make it to the promise. A delay is not always a delay; sometimes it is a denial. God is not going to force His promises on you; if you don't want what He has for you, He will respect your wishes.

What say you? Can you determine in your mind, to make it to the promise? Let's continue to read on and go on this journey together.

Lastly, there was a story about two twin boys; their father was addicted to alcohol. One never drank a day in his life; the other became addicted to alcohol. When was one twin asked how come he never became addicted to alcohol? His response was I watched my father drink my entire life. The other twin who was addicted to alcohol was asked how he became addicted to alcohol; his response was I watched my father drink my entire life. The point is it is not what happens to you, but your perception and your response that dictates whether you fail or succeed.

Chapter 2

Confidence Versus Divine Confidence

Psalm 139:14 (KJV)

14 I will praise thee; for I am fearfully and wonderfully made: marvellous are thy works; and that my soul knoweth right well.

Confidence is a feeling of self-assurance arising from one's appreciation of one's own abilities or qualities. Confidence is defined as the state of feeling certain about the truth of something. Confidence is also defined as the feeling or belief that one can rely on someone or something; firm trust. Before we go further, we have to understand what kind of confidence we need as believers. Mostly importantly confidence is always related to what we have a sense of trust, honor or high esteem in. Confidence is not some random idea that we swirl around in our head. Confidence is always related to what we put trust in. **In** is the key word here, it will make sense in a minute.

When I talk about confidence, I am not referring to the confidence as defined by the secular world. We want supernatural confidence that is only released by the Holy Spirit.

There are different types of confidence that we will discuss.

The first is self-confidence. This self-confidence is focused on self. It means when you are confident because of your ability. Self-confidence is a feeling of trust **in** one's abilities, qualities, and judgment.

Believe it or not, for the sake of this book, we are not talking about being confident in ourselves. That may sound confusing but go with me this will make sense in a minute. What God has for us has nothing to do with our ability rather what He can do through us. In Christ, we don't need to put confidence **in** ourselves.

Psalm 118:8

 It is better to **trust in** the Lord than to put confidence **in** man.

Psalm 118:9

It is better to **trust in** the Lord than to put confidence **in** princes.

Proverbs 3:26

For the Lord shall be thy confidence, and shall keep thy foot from being taken.

The reality is many people put confidence **in** many things. I remember years ago, being very disappointed in a so-called friend. It felt like the only time I heard from her was if she wanted something or needed something. I talked to God about it, and He said, "put no confidence **in** the flesh." God was telling me it was okay to not trust her deeds because of her actions.

Although we can gain a certain level of confidence in what we do, and what we accomplish. If you spent years trying to hone your craft as a singer or a writer, eventually you will be good at what you do, and thereby you would be confident **in** your gift. This isn't always a bad thing. The truth of the matter is we fail. We fail ourselves; we fail other people. If your confidence is only found **in** what you do when you fail or don't get something right, there goes your confidence right out of the door.

God doesn't want us to put confidence **in the** flesh, even our flesh. Believe it or not, our flesh cannot truly receive or understand the things of God. God's purpose puts up an invisible barrier between Him and our flesh. This is why people who have confidence only in their flesh have a hard time receiving or understanding the things of God. If we want the supernatural confidence of God to manifest we can't do it putting confidence in the flesh.

Romans 7:18 (NKJV)

18 For I know that in me (that is, in my flesh) nothing good dwells; for to will is present with me, but how to perform what is good I do not find.

Romans 8: 7 (KJV)

7 Because the carnal mind is enmity against God: for it is not subject to the law of God, neither indeed can be.

Enmity means enemy, opposed to in opposition. If your confidence is only in you, the word tells us that without Christ your mind is opposed to God.

1 Corinthians 1:25-31 Living Bible (TLB)

25 This so-called "foolish" plan of God is far wiser than the wisest plan of the wisest man, and God in his weakness— Christ dying on the cross—is far stronger than any man.

26 Notice among yourselves, dear brothers, that few of you who follow Christ have big names or power or wealth.

27 Instead, God has deliberately chosen to use ideas the world considers foolish and of little worth in order to shame those people considered by the world as wise and great.

28 He has chosen a plan despised by the world, counted as nothing at all, and used it to bring down to nothing those the world considers great,

29 so that no one anywhere can ever brag in the presence of God.

30 For it is from God alone that you have your life through Christ Jesus. He showed us God's plan of salvation; he was the one who made us acceptable to God; he made us pure and holy[a] and gave himself to purchase our salvation.*

31 As it says in the Scriptures, "If anyone is going to boast, let him boast only of what the Lord has done."

1 Corinthians 2:12-16 (TLB)

12 And God has actually given us his Spirit (not the world's spirit) to tell us about the wonderful free gifts of grace and blessing that God has given us.

13 In telling you about these gifts we have even used the very words given to us by the Holy Spirit, not words that we as

men might choose. So we use the Holy Spirit's words to explain the Holy Spirit's facts.[a]

14 But the man who isn't a Christian can't understand and can't accept these thoughts from God, which the Holy Spirit teaches us. They sound foolish to him because only those who have the Holy Spirit within them can understand what the Holy Spirit means. Others just can't take it in.

15 But the spiritual man has insight into everything, and that bothers and baffles the man of the world, who can't understand him at all.

16 How could he? For certainly he has never been one to know the Lord's thoughts, or to discuss them with him, or to move the hands of God by prayer.[b] But, strange as it seems, we Christians actually do have within us a portion of the very thoughts and mind of Christ.

The truth is if we are going to understand God confidence we must have a relationship with God, and His Holy Spirit. We cannot understand fully God, His mind, His ways, and His thoughts in our flesh.

This leads me to our discussion. What is the difference between regular confidence as the secular world defines it as versus the God kind of confidence we are addressing in this book?

First, as stated confidence is always trust in something. We said that you could be confidence in your abilities, talents, and gifts. You can be confident in other people. The secular world defines confidence as in something; the keyword is **in**, you, your ability, your accomplishments, your roles or social, economic position in life. I hope you see the pattern, the world gains confidence in something that tends you to focus on self and make the flesh feel good.

Nevertheless, God confidence has nothing to do with self or the flesh. God-confidence is complete trust, hope, and faith in God, His mind, His thoughts, His nature, His word.

This is very important because when God is preparing you for the ministry He will often allow a series of trials, so you die to yourself and your self will so you are raised in Him. The way to God-confidence is to die to the flesh.

In the secular world, you have to build yourself up. In Christ, we must deny ourselves, our flesh, our will and embrace God. When we embrace not how we feel about ourselves, but how God feels about us, and what He says about us, a divine exchange begins to happen, because our confidence is found **in** Him.

I told you briefly my story about how I suffered from poor self-confidence and poor self-worth. Even though I have accomplished a lot by man's standards, I didn't gain confidence in what I achieved. There are a lot of successful people who still have low confidence.

In years past I naively thought that if I could just accomplish this or accomplish that, then I would be happy, and then I would be confident. Well, I did just what I set my mind to do, and you know what? I was just as miserable and self-loathing as I was before I accomplished it.

I began to understand myself and building confidence when I found myself in God. Let us look at what the scripture has to say about confidence in something.

So how do we begin to get to God confidence? As stated we first must deny our flesh. Recognizing that our flesh has its own will and it wants nothing to do with God. It doesn't matter how super saved you are; your flesh has its own will. Your flesh wants to be glorified put on a pedestal. You must make a commitment to deny your flesh.

Romans 8:13 (NKJV)

13 For if you live according to the flesh you will die; but if by the Spirit you put to death the deeds of the body, you will live.

Matthew 16:24 (NKJV)

24 Then Jesus said to His disciples, "If anyone desires to come after Me, let him deny himself, and take up his cross, and follow Me.

The cross is representative of a place of self-sacrifice and self-denial. Think about it, if Jesus were confident by the world standards He would not have gotten on the cross. He would have justified His flesh. Maybe He would have affirmed His flesh, looked over the fact that He was a good person, accomplished and world renown, He didn't deserve to die. He would not have allowed His self to be put on the cross for unjust reasons.

This is what the secular definition of confidence is, it is not about self-denial but affirming of the flesh. This is why when an individual goes to seek a secular mental health counselor if they are going to help build your esteem, they don't teach you about self-denial and finding Christ, they teach you how to affirm yourself. I am not against affirmations, but if the affirmations don't lead to Christ and what He has to say about us, it is nothing more than glorifying the flesh, which is against God. We can't make our flesh an idol.

1 Corinthians 1:29-30 (KJV)

29 That no flesh should glory **in** his presence.

30 But of him are ye **in** Christ Jesus, who of God is made unto us wisdom, and righteousness, and sanctification, and redemption:

Notice the key word here is **in,** a reoccurring word we keep reading as it relates to confidence. In Christian mental health counseling, we affirm ourselves in the word of God because then we are learning to place our confidence in Him.

The next thing we must do is trust Him. We can't trust ourselves, our wit, our emotions. This is very different from this new age theology, most of it teaches us to go within ourselves, in our inner conscious to find truth and inner peace. This is nothing but a bunch of new age, psychobabble. Look at what the scripture says.

Proverbs 3:5-6 (NKJV)

5 Trust in the Lord with all your heart,

And lean not on your own understanding;

6 In all your ways acknowledge Him,

And He shall direct[a] your paths.

Remember I said confidence is another word for what we put our trust in. We could technically say, put all your confidence (trust) in the Lord, and don't lean on yourself.

I know I sound like a broken record, but do you see our word of the day? **In.**

We will talk more about the supernatural power of God but know that learning to trust God is easier said than done. Trusting God means not looking at what you see but trusting in what He said. In fact, I wrote a book years ago, Trusting God Is Not Easy But It Is Worth It.

God supernaturally empowers the believer to operate in signs and wonders once our trust is fully in Him.

To walk in divine confidence, we must forgive. The Holy Spirit will not move supernaturally in our lives when forgiveness is not present. If we cannot extend grace to others, we cannot expect God's supernatural grace to be bestowed upon us.

Matthew 18:21-33Living Bible (TLB)

21 Then Peter came to him and asked, "Sir, how often should I forgive a brother who sins against me? Seven times?"

22 "No!" Jesus replied, "seventy times seven!

23 "The Kingdom of Heaven can be compared to a king who decided to bring his accounts up to date. 24 In the process, one of his debtors was brought in who owed him $10 million!$10 million, literally, "10,000 talents." Approximately £3 million.

25 He couldn't pay, so the king ordered him sold for the debt, also his wife and children and everything he had.

26 "But the man fell down before the king, his face in the dust, and said, 'Oh, sir, be patient with me and I will pay it all.'

27 "Then the king was filled with pity for him and released him and forgave his debt.

28 "But when the man left the king, he went to a man who owed him $2,000$2,000, approximately £700. and grabbed him by the throat and demanded instant payment.

29 "The man fell down before him and begged him to give him a little time. 'Be patient and I will pay it,' he pled.

30 "But his creditor wouldn't wait. He had the man arrested and jailed until the debt would be paid in full.

31 "Then the man's friends went to the king and told him what had happened.

32 And the king called before him the man he had forgiven and said, 'You evil-hearted wretch! Here I forgave you all that tremendous debt, just because you asked me to—

33 shouldn't you have mercy on others, just as I had mercy on you?'

Lastly, we must acknowledge areas where we are broken. When a person has a hard time trusting, when they suffer from low confidence and low self-esteem, somewhere in the past there was a broken place that we never got healed from. The sad reality is that we can't gain something without losing something. We can't get without giving. We must acknowledge where we are in Christ, sometimes, many times that is not always a good place. It is hard to acknowledge where we are broken.

When I was going through my healing process, I had to have a heart to heart talk with Jesus. I told Him I knew what His word says in my head, but my heart was having a hard time. I knew I struggled with trusting God. Growing up I never knew a true authentic father's love, even though I was raised in the church. I had to learn to accept God's love for me which would then in time transform how I saw God and then myself.

Beloved God won't heal you from a hurt you won't acknowledge.

There is a place in God that you will walk in boldness, fearless, being a mighty warrior for Him. It starts with knowing and acknowledging that you need God-confidence. Let's go on, let the process begin.

Chapter 3

Holy Boldness

Acts 1:8 (KJV)

8 But ye shall receive power, after that the Holy Ghost is come upon you: and ye shall be witnesses unto me both in Jerusalem, and in all Judaea, and in Samaria, and unto the uttermost part of the earth.

Imagine getting up to speak or sing to thousands of people. You may be very nervous; if you're like me, you are more than nervous. Maybe you have never spoken in front of such a large audience, maybe you have. Any great speaker will tell you no matter how many times you speak, right before there is a little bit of nervousness that will be present. It is perfectly normal. Nevertheless, this time when you get up to speak, something supernatural happens. You speak but you are operating in such boldness and divine confidence you don't recognize yourself. You are speaking on a whole new level. No fear is present just boldness. This is the work of the Holy Spirit. He gives us the power to be a bold witness for him.

This is what happened on the day of Pentecost. Peter who was a disciple of Jesus had previously denied knowing Jesus, even though they were very close. Why did he do that? It wasn't that he didn't love Jesus it was because of fear. Jesus had been taken off to be persecuted and die. It appeared as though life was falling apart, and Peter was afraid of dying.

Isn't that just like fear? Fear will cause us to run away from the very thing God wants us to move towards. God is awesome. We thank Him for grace and forgiveness. Jesus knew the part that fear would play in Peter's life. Despite Peter's declaration of his willingness to fight for Jesus, his heart and motives were in the right place; his flesh had some other ideas.

Matthew 26:31-35 (TLB)

31 Then Jesus said to them, "Tonight you will all desert me. For it is written in the Scriptures[a] that God will smite the Shepherd, and the sheep of the flock will be scattered.

32 But after I have been brought back to life again, I will go to Galilee and meet you there."

33 Peter declared, "If everyone else deserts you, I won't."

34 Jesus told him, "The truth is that this very night, before the cock crows at dawn, you will deny me three times!"

35 "I would die first!" Peter insisted. And all the other disciples said the same thing.

Later on.......

Matthew 26:69-74 (TLB)

69 Meanwhile, as Peter was sitting in the courtyard, a girl came over and said to him, "You were with Jesus, for both of you are from Galilee."[a]

70 But Peter denied it loudly. "I don't even know what you are talking about," he angrily declared.

71 Later, out by the gate, another girl noticed him and said to those standing around, "This man was with Jesus—from Nazareth."

72 Again Peter denied it, this time with an oath. "I don't even know the man," he said.

73 But after a while the men who had been standing there came over to him and said, "We know you are one of his disciples, for we can tell by your Galilean[b] accent."

74 Peter began to curse and swear. "I don't even know the man," he said.

And immediately the cock crowed.

My point is not for us to look down on Peter. The reality is we all have a Peter on the inside of us. We are like Peter we want to go hard for Jesus. We mean well, but when chaos breaks loose, and we are in trouble our well-meaning words may mean another thing.

Therefore we need the supernatural ability of the Holy Spirit. He empowers us to be witnesses for Jesus without the fear of man. Fear will present itself no matter who you are. The world will persecute you for your true alliance with Christ. You can't be afraid to die for Jesus; we need supernatural boldness. That leads us to our text found in Acts 2, and back to are beloved disciple Peter.

First, before Jesus ascended into heaven, He promised the disciples that they wouldn't be left alone but the Holy Spirit would come.

John 14:15-17 Living Bible (TLB)

15-16 "If you love me, obey me; and I will ask the Father and he will give you another Comforter, and he will never leave you.

17 He is the Holy Spirit, the Spirit who leads into all truth. The world at large cannot receive him, for it isn't looking for him and doesn't recognize him. But you do, for he lives with you now and some day shall be in you.

The Comforter is the Holy Spirit. He has different functions and to help us do the ministry of Christ. Yet, one main function of the Holy Spirit is to empower us to be witnesses for Him.

Acts 1:7-8 (KJV)

7 And he said unto them, It is not for you to know the times or the seasons, which the Father hath put in his own power.

8 But ye shall receive power, after that the Holy Ghost comes upon you: and ye shall be witnesses unto me both in Jerusalem, and in all Judaea, and in Samaria, and unto the uttermost part of the earth.

Jesus was saying we don't know when the Holy Spirit is going to come, but when He comes, He is going to give us the power to be a witness. Power is the supernatural ability to accomplish heaven's agenda. A witness is the power to testify. It means a person who sees or otherwise has personal knowledge of something.

You see the reason why Peter denied Jesus was because he didn't have the supernatural power to be a witness for Jesus.

So, when he was asked about him, his flesh did what only flesh can do when it is afraid, run, deny knowing who he is.

Then the day of Pentecost came just as Jesus promised. The supernatural happened.

Acts 2:1-17 (NKJV)

1 When the Day of Pentecost had fully come, they were all with one accord[a] in one place.

2 And suddenly there came a sound from heaven, as of a rushing mighty wind, and it filled the whole house where they were sitting.

3 Then there appeared to them divided tongues, as of fire, and one sat upon each of them. 4 And they were all filled with the Holy Spirit and began to speak with other tongues, as the Spirit gave them utterance.

The Crowd's Response

5 And there were dwelling in Jerusalem Jews, devout men, from every nation under heaven.

6 And when this sound occurred, the multitude came together, and were confused, because everyone heard them speak in his own language.

7 Then they were all amazed and marveled, saying to one another, "Look, are not all these who speak Galileans?

8 And how is it that we hear, each in our own language in which we were born?

9 Parthians and Medes and Elamites, those dwelling in Mesopotamia, Judea and Cappadocia, Pontus and Asia,

10 Phrygia and Pamphylia, Egypt and the parts of Libya adjoining Cyrene, visitors from Rome, both Jews and proselytes, 11 Cretans and Arabs—we hear them speaking in our own tongues the wonderful works of God." 12 So they were all amazed and perplexed, saying to one another, "Whatever could this mean?"

13 Others mocking said, "They are full of new wine."

Peter's Sermon

14 But Peter, standing up with the eleven, raised his voice and said to them, "Men of Judea and all who dwell in Jerusalem, let this be known to you, and heed my words.

15 For these are not drunk, as you suppose, since it is only the third hour of the day.

16 But this is what was spoken by the prophet Joel:

17 'And it shall come to pass in the last days, says God,

That I will pour out of My Spirit on all flesh;

Your sons and your daughters shall prophesy,

Your young men shall see visions,

Your old men shall dream dreams.

It is believed that 120 people were in a room waiting on the promise of the Holy Spirit to come. Pentecost came about 17 weeks after Jesus death and ascension into heaven. That is a little more than four months after Jesus left. I want you to see Peter's response after the Holy Spirit manifest. After the Holy Spirit came, Peter is now speaking boldly to hundreds of people that turned into thousands.

Acts 2:40-47 (NKJV)

40 And with many other words he testified and exhorted them, saying, "Be saved from this perverse generation."

41 Then those who gladly[a] received his word were baptized; and that day about **three thousand souls** were added to them.

42 And they continued steadfastly in the apostles' doctrine and fellowship, in the breaking of bread, and in prayers.

43 Then fear came upon every soul, and many wonders and signs were done through the apostles.

44 Now all who believed were together, and had all things in common,

45 and sold their possessions and goods, and divided them among all, as anyone had need.

46 So continuing daily with one accord in the temple, and breaking bread from house to house, they ate their food with gladness and simplicity of heart,

47 praising God and having favor with all the people. And the Lord added to the church[b] daily those who were being saved.

The Holy Spirit fell, supernatural manifestation came. This same Peter who was scared and frightened even to acknowledge he knew Jesus then gets up and boldly declares the word of God, to the point where the first church was established and in one day they went from 120 people waiting in a room, to three thousand people. Not only is he now speaking powerfully, other people with him began to testify of Jesus. Where did Peter's fear go? Remember I said this wasn't years later, this was four months. Most therapist will tell you it takes years to develop into this level of confidence. Here is Peter and many like him boldly declaring the word of God, without fear. What happened? The supernatural power of the Holy Spirit came.

Four things that happen when the supernatural power of God comes;

1. Fear leaves and supernatural boldness comes.
2. Supernatural increase comes, remember they went from one hundred and twenty people to three thousand people.
3. You are supernaturally empowered to accomplish the agenda of heaven, through Christ.
4. Supernatural healing and deliverance begin to take place.

I don't know about you, but that makes me excited. Hopefully, you are seeing the difference in the secular world you gain confidence in you. In Christ, we gain confidence in Him, empowered supernaturally by the Holy Spirit. Let's look at another example.

Acts 4:13-16 (NKJV)

13 Now when they saw the boldness of Peter and John, and perceived that they were uneducated and untrained men, they marveled. And they realized that they had been with Jesus.

14 And seeing the man who had been healed standing with them, they could say nothing against it.

15 But when they had commanded them to go aside out of the council, they conferred among themselves,

16 saying, "What shall we do to these men? For, indeed, that a notable miracle has been done through them is evident to all who dwell in Jerusalem, and we cannot deny it

Acts 4:21 (NKJV)

21 So when they had further threatened them, they let them go, finding no way of punishing them, because of the people, since they all glorified God for what had been done.

Acts 4:29-31 (NKJV)

29 Now, Lord, look on their threats, and grant to Your servants that with all boldness they may speak Your word,

30 by stretching out Your hand to heal, and that signs and wonders may be done through the name of Your holy Servant Jesus."

31 And when they had prayed, the place where they were assembled together was shaken; and they were all filled with the Holy Spirit, and they spoke the word of God with boldness.

The devil does not want you to operate in boldness. So, after Pentecost, great persecution began. Peter has just been released from prison because of speaking the word of God. Notice the Holy Spirit doesn't stop the persecution from coming, He stops you from fearing it. This same Peter who denied Jesus is now speaking the word of God boldly. Hopefully, you see the transformation that takes place in Peter's life. He is being put in prison, his life is threatened, yet he still is speaking the word of God. Fear is gone from him.

Notice that believers started being persecuted. Being a Christian and declaring the word of God makes you controversial. I love how they prayed. Look at what the scripture in Acts does say and what it doesn't say. Notice they didn't pray for the persecution to end. They didn't pray for their enemy's demise. They specifically prayed for boldness to speak the word of God despite the threats and the Holy Spirit responded.

Beloved when you determine to advance God's kingdom and speak boldly for Jesus the devil is mad. The Holy Spirit empowers us to be a witness for Him. If you ask God for boldness, He will give it just like in the days of Acts.

Part II: Destiny Killers

Chapter 4

Rejection, Insecurity, and Impotence

1 Samuel 18:7 (NKJV)

7 So the women sang as they danced, and said:

"Saul has slain his thousands,

And David his ten thousands."

We must take a step back and discuss what robs people of their confidence. This is so important. We have discussed the workings of the Holy Spirit to give us supernatural boldness to be a witness for Him. Yet, the reality is there are many Christians who are filled with the baptism of the Holy Spirit, with evidence of speaking in tongues, yet they are defeated, they suffer from low self-esteem and have no power. We must know and understand why. The Holy Spirit is a gentleman. He will not force His power on us. We must know and understand how the enemy creeps in and disarms us of our God-given power.

The enemy wants Christians to be defeated. He doesn't want you to walk in the divine authority of who God has created you to be. It is like having the keys to a brand-new car. You have the keys. You are the rightful owner, yet if you don't know you have the keys. If you don't know what your rights are, you still have no power. You are still walking, when you could be riding in luxury. Beloved having the keys to the kingdom of God is one thing, being able to use them is another thing.

We must look at how the enemy plants seeds of dissension that robs us of confidence. First, we know that often many people who have low confidence have a bad start in life. We must look at how a spirit of rejection contributes significantly to having low confidence.

Rejection simply means to be refused. It means to be denied. Rejection means to refuse to accept, consider, submit to, take for some purpose. Let's be honest rejection hurts; no one wants to be rejected. No one wants to be rejected at any level, yet we all have experienced rejection at some point and time. Even God Himself has experienced rejection from His people. There is no need to run from rejection; rather we must have a clear understanding of who we are, our identity in God and His love towards us.

Rejection can begin at different places in life. Nevertheless, most people don't know that rejection can begin in the wound. Some call this prenatal rejection. It is sad to think, but some babies will come out of the wound feeling rejected. This happened when there are difficult circumstances surrounding the conception. If the mother was an unwed woman who never wanted children, it could be the parents wanted a boy, but they got a girl. If the mother conceived because of rape. There are so many reasons why a baby can come out with the spirit of rejection.

When a person struggles with a spirit of rejection, it can have devastating effects on their life. You can't truly walk in the divine favor of God when you struggle with the fruit of rejection. What is sad is that when a person struggles with the fruit of rejection eventually, they come to reject God. Although most people would never admit that they rejected God, in the subconscious mind they do.

Whenever God declares a promise over your life, or He tells you who He has called you to be and you refute that belief you are rejecting the promises of God and what He has to say about you. Often it is very difficult to walk in divine relationship with God when we struggle with the fruit of rejection. We often believe how people see us is how God sees us. If people reject us then we assume that God feels the same way and that He has rejected us.

Symptoms that a person struggles with the fruit of rejection.

1. When a person isolates.

2. Inability to communicate. When a person cannot communicate they secretly fear if they speak up even when they are being mistreated they will be rejected.

3. Attention seeking behaviors, or they are very clingy.

4. Any person that needs constant reassuring is struggling with the root of rejection.

5. Being easily offended.

6. Overly concerned about how people will perceive them. Often these people suffer from depression and anxiety because they isolate and worry.

7. Perfectionism.

8. Overachieving, (performance driven) this individual is always working towards excellence to seek approval.

9.Constantly complaining.

10.Inability to receive critic (constructive criticism).

11.Believes no one understands them.

12.Having to prove oneself.

12.Anyone who is abusive suffers from a history of rejection.

13.A history of broken relationships. If everywhere you go there is some drama, and you are the common denominator, you maybe the problem.

14.Difficulty is cultivating authentic relationships.

15.Inability to take a compliment.

16.Inability to be emotionally intimate with someone.

17.Surface conversations. These people never go deep in conversation because of fear.

18.Keeping people at an emotional distance for fear of rejection.

Rejection breeds insecurity. You can't have a truly authentic relationship with people when you struggle with the fruit of rejection. You can't have an authentic relationship with God when you struggle with rejection. You can't walk in divine confidence when rejection is present.

In another chapter, we will talk about how rejection impacts your ability to lead and creates what we call, a perverted sonship. Hang in there this chapter is setting the foundation for us to go to heavier topics in our upcoming chapters.

Rejection breeds insecurity. Breed means to reproduce after its kind. Insecurity means uncertainty or anxiety about oneself; lack of confidence. Insecurity is the state of being open to danger or threat; lack of protection.

Have you ever been in a relationship with someone who is insecure? It is torture. Insecurity ruins relationships, it prevents divine connections. At the beginning of the chapter, we read a quote from the life of King Saul and David I want to revisit this to point out how insecurity negatively impacts us. Let's read the text together.

We should know the story by now, but Saul has been rejected as king due to his disobedience. By the way, you can't fulfill the plan and purpose that God has for your life when you intentionally disobey him. Saul was warned, he did it again, God responded. God's response was not what Saul wanted to hear.

As time goes on, God sent Prophet Samuel to anoint another king. God chose David. David had to be trained up to be a king. Ironically God places David in the home of Saul. Saul has no idea that technically David is his replacement, all he knows is there is a young boy, who plays the harp that eases his mental illness.

Sounds like a good situation for David. David had father wounds; he was rejected by his biological father; his brothers didn't like him. Now David is living with the king. Not only is he living with a king, but he also found favor with the king. Saul has adopted David like a son. In fact, when you look at the interactions between King Saul and David, David would often refer to Saul as "my father." Isn't that wonderful?

You've been rejected all your life, by your father and your brothers, but look at God. Again, sounds great right. Well not so much, the story continues. David gets close to Saul and Saul's children. He is like one of the kids. Saul's son Johnathan and David become best friends, Saul's daughter also falls in love with David. David has it made. So, we think.

David kept his secret about one day being a king; he is just enjoying his time in the palace. The teacher in me can't just give you the story without a scriptural reference; I encourage you to read the story of the interaction between David and Saul on your own. I am going to quote one text. Also see 1 Samuel 15:19-23. For our text, we will read I Samuel

1 Samuel 16:21-23 (NKJV)

21 So David came to Saul and stood before him. And he loved him greatly, and he became his armorbearer.

22 Then Saul sent to Jesse, saying, "Please let David stand before me, for he has found favor in my sight."

23 And so it was, whenever the spirit from God was upon Saul, that David would take a harp and play it with his hand. Then Saul would become refreshed and well, and the distressing spirit would depart from him.

David has it made in the shade. I believe that David struggled with rejection, the difference is once David was anointed as king, God declared a blessing over his life. He chose to believe what God had to say about him. I believe God used Saul and his family to heal the fruit of rejection that he experienced from his earthly father and his biological brothers. David had no issues with Saul and only wanted to honor him as his leader and spiritual father. David wasn't just going to walk into his position within the kingdom easily. No he wasn't just going to serve Saul until Saul died. He had to be processed. So how did such a great relationship turn so ugly? Saul ended up having homicidal ideations with a plan and intent to kill. Ideations mean thoughts.

Ironically the man that David came to love ended up being his arch enemy number one, and he did nothing wrong. We will follow this story in greater detail in another chapter called When Father' Kill. I simply want to point out how insecurity comes in. Saul is a king mighty in battle. He has won many battles.

Then there comes along Goliath. Someone that Saul couldn't conquer. David had experienced killing lions, tigers and bears when he was at his home, tending sheep. He volunteers to kill Goliath. Saul probably laughed at him and thought he was as good as dead. He probably humored the young boy by letting him go to fight Goliath. We are in I Samuel 1. You should know the story. David goes to fight Goliath. Goliath is so arrogant he laughs, at this little boy trying to fight him. I Samuel 17:43. Goliath was insulted that David came out to fight.

1 Samuel 17:43 Living Bible (TLB)

43 "Am I a dog," he (Goliath) roared at David, "that you come at me with a stick?" And he cursed David by the names of his gods.

It is important to note that when God is on your side, there is no Goliath, no mountain, no obstacle that is too big for you. You know the story David defeats Goliath, kills him. David gets a newfound, notoriety that he didn't ask for. He didn't go to fight to become famous he went to fight to defeat the enemies of God.

Whenever someone is seeking notoriety, self-promotion, and fame their heart is not for God. Believe it or not, they struggle with low self-esteem no matter how confident they appear. These individuals are seeking validation from sources outside of themselves. Don't pursue fame, fortune or notoriety pursue God.

To make a long story short now Saul's love turned to hatred because of David's success. People ended up comparing David and Saul. Saul over hears a song that the people have come up with. The lyrics go, "Saul has slain his thousands, and David his ten thousand."

Apparently, Saul didn't like the song. David didn't make up the song. Insecurity always breeds envy, a feeling of discontentment or resentful longing aroused by someone else's possessions, qualities, or luck.

Here is this young boy, coming from seemly out of nowhere, and now the people have proclaimed David to be better than Saul.

When a person is insecure, they can't celebrate another person. Insecurity breeds comparison. Don't ever compare yourself to another person. Comparison is to look at (two or more things) closely to see what is similar or different about them or to decide which one is better.

The difference between Saul and David was that David's heart was towards God. Saul's heart was towards his self and his self-motives which was his pattern all along.

People will compare you to another person. Some people have their likes and dislikes. I have two sisters, growing up they were always outgoing, and I was the quiet one. They had friends and were popularity I had my books. I was always compared to them. In my immaturity, I would often think something was wrong with me, because I was introverted, and they were extraverted. Eventually, as God healed my heart I realized I was just the person I was supposed to be, they were just the person they were supposed to be, and that was that. I don't want to be them, and they don't want to be me. I am not jealous or envious of them and vice versa. People have their preferences; one may like my sister's personality more than mine and vice versa that is life. My point is if Saul's heart were in the right place he wouldn't have taken the words to heart. If he were confident in who he was he wouldn't care how people saw him.

When you know who you are, you just realize some people are not going to like you; some people will, that's life. Funny story. A few months ago, a friend of mine wanted to introduce me to a guy she had just met. She described him to me I was initially intrigued. He contacted me; we exchanged numbers. We talked for a bit; I thought we had a lot in common. However, he was very guarded, standoffish and appeared very passive. He didn't pursue to get to know me at all. I was not impressed, after the first conversation I was done. Still, I gave him grace, talked to him two more times and then I was still done. My friend was telling me he was just shy and needed time. I knew she wanted me to hit it off with him, but I was not feeling it. A passive, guarded man, nope I don't think so. I am too old for that. To make a long story short as it turns out he wanted to get comfortable with my friend in a way that was inappropriate. Ironically my friend is a Christian, married with three kids. He was well aware of this and still tried to her to connect out with her. She was not having it in the least.

My point if I weren't a secure person I would feel some kind of way about this, but I don't. I know I am a beautiful person, he doesn't deserve my time. He clearly has issues with rejection, insecurity and discerning what appropriate versus inappropriate boundaries are.

Sometimes God orchestrates rejection for our good. Any man that doesn't respect the boundaries of a married woman is not the kind of man that I want to be friends with let alone in a relationship with.

Jesus was rejected. Maybe if David had not been rejected, he would have gotten comfortable in his position as an armor bearer in the king's house instead of the king.

It is important to note that rejection is a season (series) of test that God ordains for anyone called to ministry. You must pass the test of rejection. Every leader within the bible had a season of rejection. You name it (Abraham, Moses, David, Joseph, Jesus). Rejection hurts when it comes from people that we are trying to help, or from people we love the most.

We must take a different perspective on rejection. Rejection is preparation for ministry. When God brings you to a place of success, your motivating factor can't be how well people will like you. You'll end of being motivated by selfish gain for the applause of people. What if God wants you to say things in love, and truth that others don't want to hear? We need real sanctified saints in this day and hour.

Rejection, insecurity left unchecked, and not delivered creates spiritual impotence. When I say impotence, I am not referring to what you may think. Spiritual impotence both men and women can suffer from. Spiritual impotence means an inability to act or helplessness. Eventually they cannot be productive, they become weak, lack power and ability these individuals resolve is to spend their days in a defeated position. There is no such thing as a little bit of rejection or a little bit of fear, or a little bit of insecurity. No, it all breeds, it is like cancer, it may start in one part of the body but left untreated it will consume the entire body and thereby rob us of our very life. God can't use a weak-minded Christian that refuses to allow the virtue of the Holy Spirit to refill them.

We must gain mastery over our emotions. We must cast down vain imaginations and anything that puts us outside of the will of God. You must be intentional about your deliverance.

Do you want to walk in divine confidence? One exercise that I have my clients do is to pick a life scripture and for the next 21 days begin to recite that scripture. This is not a one size fits all to build confidence, but it does put us in the right direction. We will talk about about strategies to build God-confidence in a later chapter.

Example of scriptures to recite:

Psalm 139:14 (NKJV)

14 I will praise You, for I am fearfully and wonderfully made;[a]

Marvelous are Your works,

And that my soul knows very well.

Psalm 118:6 (NKJV)

6 The Lord is on my side;

I will not fear.

What can man do to me?

Philippians 4:13 (NKJV)

13 I can do all things through Christ[a] who strengthens me.

You must begin to speak over your life. When you begin to speak, it has nothing to do with feelings. You can say these things about you, and you don't have to believe them. You just keep speaking the word of God, out loud. Eventually, your mind and your heart begin to cooperate. You begin to believe what God has to say about you.

Yet even with all of that if you are in denial about where you are insecure, have a fruit of rejection, that is leaving you powerless you will not be able to get free. Denial and repression don't get you to the promise.

Chapter 5

A Fatherless Generation

Malachi 4:6 (NKJV)

6 And he will turn

The hearts of the fathers to the children,

And the hearts of the children to their fathers,

Lest I come and strike the earth with a curse. "

We must get to the root of why many Christian's have low confidence. We discussed in the past how the spirit of rejection could play a major role in why many have low confidence. Nevertheless, it is important that we uncover and expose a major agenda of the enemy. Again, satan doesn't want you to understand who you are in him. He does have a strategy and plans to defeat us. We are in a battle. The wonderful news is if we stick with Christ we do indeed win.

Ephesians 6:12 (NKJV)

12 For we do not wrestle against flesh and blood, but against principalities, against powers, against the rulers of the darkness of this age,[a] against spiritual hosts of wickedness in the heavenly places.

Anyone knows that before you go into battle, you must know the strategy of the enemy. Deciding to not fight by default puts you in the defeated category.

When a person has the root of rejection, insecurity, envious, jealousy, they are not clear about their identity in God. That leads us to discuss the enemies plot against the father.

First, let's discuss the role of the father. The father's role is to provide, protect and to give identity. If you ask anyone who has had a great relationship with their father, somewhere in the conversation the father was a great provider, protector and gave them their identity. The secret agenda is to rob the earth of the father. Satan hates the father. The first reason he hates the role of the father is that it was Father God who created the earth. When God created man, He created him to reflect the very nature of who He is. When satan seeks to attack the father and the father role it is his way of intentionally trying to come against the plan of God.

God wants to use the role of the father to restore us back to our rightful positions as kingdom citizens.

Unfortunately, satan has been successful in many ways of robing an entire generation of the father. Statically speaking we know this to be true. According to the Washington Times, although as a country we added 160,000 new families with children, the number of two-parent households decreased by 1.2 million. Fifteen million U.S. children, or 1 in 3, live without a father, and nearly 5 million live without a mother. In 1960, just 11 percent of American children lived in homes without fathers. Dec 25, 2012

Fathers disappear from households across America - Washington Times. https://www.washingtontimes.com/.../fathers-disappear-from-households-across-america/Retrieved on January 1, 2018

There are multiple generations that have been robbed of the father.

When there is a lack of a father in this generation what we create is a generation of individuals who lack identity or give themselves a false identity. Look what scripture says about our identity in God.

Psalm 100:3 (NKJV)

3 Know that the Lord, He is God;

It is He who has made us, and not we ourselves;[a]

We are His people and the sheep of His pasture.

Genesis 5:2 (NKJV)

2 He created them male and female, and blessed them and called them Mankind in the day they were created.

Notice God created us; we didn't create ourselves. He created us to be male or female. We are not permitted to recreate our gender, to be gender neutral or to change our gender identity. No matter how many operations a person gets, they will either be male or female in the eyes of God and according to the DNA. This LGBT movement seeks to have individuals redefine their identity that God gave them. This is out of order and out of the will of God.

There is no mistake that the LGBT movement is getting stronger because they are trying to advance the agenda of the enemy satan.

Other roles of the father include operating in authority, governmental rule, headship, dominion, power, and respect. When you know who you are in God the Father, He releases Holy Spirit which empowers us in this way. Most importantly we have power over satan and his entire demonic kingdom.

Let's look further at the plot of the enemy. It is important to note that satan is not that smart, he does the same thing repeatedly. Generations may change, people live and die, but his tactics stay the same.

Exodus 1:22 (NKJV)

22 So Pharaoh commanded all his people, saying, "Every son who is born[a] you shall cast into the river, and every daughter you shall save alive."

Why did Pharaoh want innocent babies, particularly males? Something is wrong when you want to kill innocent babies. Two words insecurity and jealousy.

Exodus 1:9-22Living Bible (TLB)

9 He told his people, "These Israelis are becoming dangerous to us because there are so many of them.

10 Let's figure out a way to put an end to this. If we don't, and war breaks out, they will join our enemies and fight against us and escape out of the country."

11 So the Egyptians made slaves of them and put brutal taskmasters over them to wear them down under heavy burdens while building the cities of Pithom and Rameses as supply centers for the king.

12 But the more the Egyptians mistreated and oppressed them, the more the Israelis seemed to multiply! The Egyptians became alarmed

13-14 and made the Hebrew slavery more bitter still, forcing them to toil long and hard in the fields and to carry heavy loads of mortar and brick.

15-16 Then Pharaoh, the king of Egypt, instructed the Hebrew midwives (their names were Shiphrah and Puah) to kill all Hebrew boys as soon as they were born, but to let the girls live.

17 But the midwives feared God and didn't obey the king—they let the boys live too.

18 The king summoned them before him and demanded, "Why have you disobeyed my command and let the baby boys live?"

19 "Sir," they told him, "the Hebrew women have their babies so quickly that we can't get there in time! They are not slow like the Egyptian women!"

20 And God blessed the midwives because they were God-fearing women.[a] So the people of Israel continued to multiply and to become a mighty nation.

21 And because the midwives revered God, he gave them children of their own.

22 Then Pharaoh commanded all of his people to throw the newborn Hebrew boys into the Nile River. But the girls, he said, could live.

Therefore, it is so important to get delivered from the spirit of jealousy, and envy. Anytime someone intentionally tries to sabotage your efforts to succeed a demonic agenda of satan is involved. Notice it didn't say that the people of Israel plotted against the Pharaoh or his people. It didn't say there was a war; he just thought that he would be dethroned. He saw the people of Israel increasing, and he became afraid. Isn't that what happened to Saul when he saw David beginning to succeed? Again, remember I said satan doesn't change his method. Ironically, he tried this same strategy again thousands of years later.

Matthew 2:1-18Living Bible (TLB)

2 Jesus was born in the town of Bethlehem, in Judea, during the reign of King Herod.

At about that time some astrologers from eastern lands arrived in Jerusalem, asking,

2 "Where is the newborn King of the Jews? for we have seen his star in far-off eastern lands and have come to worship him."

3 King Herod was deeply disturbed by their question, and all Jerusalem was filled with rumors.[a]

4 He called a meeting of the Jewish religious leaders.

"Did the prophets tell us where the Messiah would be born?" he asked.

5 "Yes, in Bethlehem," they said, "for this is what the prophet Micah[b] wrote:

6 'O little town of Bethlehem, you are not just an unimportant Judean village, for a Governor shall rise from you to rule my people Israel.'"

7 Then Herod sent a private message to the astrologers, asking them to come to see him; at this meeting he found out from them the exact time when they first saw the star. Then he told them, 8 "Go to Bethlehem and search for the child. And when you find him, come back and tell me so that I can go and worship him too!"

9 After this interview the astrologers started out again. And look! The star appeared to them again, standing over Bethlehem.[c]

10 Their joy knew no bounds!

11 Entering the house where the baby and Mary, his mother, were, they threw themselves down before him, worshiping. Then they opened their presents and gave him gold, frankincense, and myrrh.

12 But when they returned to their own land, they didn't go through Jerusalem to report to Herod, for God had warned them in a dream to go home another way.

13 After they were gone, an angel of the Lord appeared to Joseph in a dream. "Get up and flee to Egypt with the baby and his mother," the angel said, "and stay there until I tell you to return, for King Herod is going to try to kill the child."

14 That same[d] night he left for Egypt with Mary and the baby,

15 and stayed there until King Herod's death. This fulfilled the prophet's prediction,

"I have called my Son from Egypt."[e]

16 Herod was furious when he learned that the astrologers had disobeyed him. Sending soldiers to Bethlehem, he ordered them to kill every baby boy two years old and under, both in the town and on the nearby farms, for the astrologers had told him the star first appeared to them two years before.

17 This brutal action of Herod's fulfilled the prophecy of Jeremiah,

18 "Screams of anguish come from Ramah,[f]

Weeping unrestrained;

Rachel weeping for her children,

Uncomforted—

For they are dead."

Hopefully, you see the similarities in the text between Moses life and Jesus life. Notice again the motivating factor for Herod was fear and intimidation. Also note the attack on male children. Once he heard a rumor about "the king of the Jews." Herod assumed that there would be some attempt to dethrone him. Isn't it ironic that both deliverers came out of Egypt?

My point is we must look at scripture to understand the agenda of satan. Thousands of years later his plot is the same; we are just in a different generation. There is still a demonic war going around.

Why? Because male sons become fathers, fathers become kings in their homes, in their world. When there is a generation that is fatherless our world then creates a generation of men who don't walk in their God-given authority, and the earth has no identity. Satan is angry at their position of authority, so he sends out his agenda just like he did in the bible times. The earth knows when sons are not present in the earth.

Romans 8:18-19 (NKJV)

18 For I consider that the sufferings of this present time are not worthy to be compared with the glory which shall be revealed in us.

19 For the earnest expectation of the creation eagerly waits for the revealing of the sons of God.

The wonderful thing about God is that He is not ignorant of satan's plots. According to the word of God, God is going to restore the hearts of the father back into position with their son's and daughter's. Let's read Malachi from The Living Bible Translation

Malachi 4:6 (TLB)

6 His preaching will bring fathers and children together again, to be of one mind and heart, for they will know that if they do not repent, I will come and utterly destroy their land."

Finally, before we move forward, we have to discuss what happens to our confidence when we grow up in homes without fathers. What is created is father wounds.

What happens when a man doesn't have a strong male figure in his life;

•A passive man

•Submitted to a controlling woman. (Often with women who has a title of Prophetess or Prophet)

•Feminized man

•Won't lead even in conversation he expects a woman to lead.

•Ahab doesn't speak up for his wife and children.

•Ahab is not a provider or protector. He can't give identity because he doesn't know his own identity. (Ahab is not a father figure)

•Compromising

•Quiet but not discerning

•No boundaries

•Intimidated by godly men. Doesn't have good male remodels or father figures to fill in the gap of his fatherlessness.

•Easily manipulated

•Doesn't speak up when wronged.

•Co-dependent (can't think for himself)

•A generational spirit (his father and grandfather are where Ahab's.)

•Didn't have good male role model's growing up, didn't have a strong father or father figure.

•Use to women taking care of him.

•Secretly suffers from anxiety, depression and chronic fear.

•Lacks leadership skills or the anointing of a leader but has a position or title of a leader.

•Is not discerning

•Doesn't like to be confronted with the truth, when he is confronted he will easily agree to avoid conflict but never changes his behavior because his heart doesn't change.

•Will easily put up with a controlling, manipulative woman.

•Expects a woman to take care of him.

•Is attracted to spiritual Jezebel's but not spiritual Esther's.

•Easily intimidated by a strong woman, while in a relationship with Jezebel (is secretly scared of her).

•May have a position, title or platform, but behind the scenes, Jezebel is running the show.

•Will sit at home sleeping while his woman works.

•Doesn't work or can't stay on a job for a long time.

•If single he goes from house to house with different women taking care of him.

•His mother was a Jezebel.

•His mother doesn't see a potential wife for her son as a potential daughter but rather someone to compete with. His mother took care of him much longer than she should have. He is an adult child.

•Came from a single parent household.

•Fear of confrontation.

•Fear of speaking the truth.

•Fear of rejection, insecure.

•Surface conversations.

Based on the symptoms present when there are father wounds a person can't operate in divine confidence when unresolved father wounds are present. No worries God has the final say.

Don't worry men I didn't leave the women out. There is a devastating consequence when a woman doesn't have a good father or father figure in her life.

•(For females) constantly comparing yourself with, and competing against, other females

•Sabotaging yourself when you experience happiness or success

•Possessing weak boundaries and an inability to say "no."

•Self-blaming and low self-esteem that manifests itself as the core belief: "There is something wrong with me."

•Co-dependency in relationships

Minimizing yourself to be likable and accepted

•The inability to speak up authentically and express your emotions fully

•Sacrificing your dreams and desires for other people unnecessarily

•Waiting for your mother's permission on an unconscious level to live life truly

https://lonerwolf.com/healing-the-mother-wound/

Other signs of mother wounds include:

•Damaged emotions

•Inability to show affection.

•You maybe harsh, cold or indifferent.

•Inability to hug, say "I love you."

•Maybe drawn to the same sex, seeking the mother's attention in a perverted way.

•Difficulty embracing your feminine nature as a woman.

•Overly dependent

•Intense anger.

•Intense fear

•Independent ("having an I don't need anybody mentality")

•Very low self-esteem

•Struggles with depression and anxiety

•May seek love through unhealthy means such as drugs, alcohol, illicit sex.

•Maybe overly masculine, may even dress like a man.

•Inability to embrace or relate to other women.

•She becomes overly submissive or controlling

•Mean argumentative.

•Jezebel

•Codependent

•Maybe sexually promiscuous

•May seek the love of a father in sexual conquest or older men.

•Lack of identity, low self-esteem

•Driven my performance

•Anxiety, depression.

•Feels unsafe

•Not discerning

•Difficulty in making wise decisions when it comes to a potential mate.

•Low confidence

•Hyper-reactive

•Very passive

•Inability to set boundaries

•Clingy

I don't care what society says or how advanced they get we need fathers in our world. Let's continue. By the way, we will talk about the restoration of the father in a later chapter.

Chapter 6

Discerning Ahab

1 Kings 16:33(KJV)

33 And Ahab made a grove; and Ahab did more to provoke the Lord God of Israel to anger than all the kings of Israel that were before him.

We must continue to uncover the agenda of the enemy to get free and walk in divine confidence. Unfortunately, in today's society, things are not always what they seem. We are living in a world where there is a spiritual undercurrent in the lives of many. There is a demonic spirit, an agenda from satan himself emasculating the man and positioning the world for the spirit of Jezebel to reign supreme. Both the spirit of Ahab and Jezebel exist today.

A few years ago, the Lord told me to begin to study the spirit of Ahab. I did, I realized that this spirit is present in many Christians today, both men and women.

There is much teaching on the spirit of Jezebel; there is not as much teaching on the spirit of Ahab. For those who are unaware Ahab was a king, therefore, he had a position of authority, and he operated in a very passive spirit. Because of his passive spirit, a nation was almost destroyed.

Ahab and Jezebel are dead, but their spirit lives today. We are seeing more and more Ahab's and Jezebel's in our world. This chapter is about how to discern the spirit of Ahab.

Although the spirit of Ahab does exist in women, it is not easily detected because it is a feminized spirit. Yet, for the sake of this chapter, we will focus on how to discern the spirit of Ahab in a man. Ironically the same symptoms that we discussed in our previous chapter where we pointed out what happens when a man doesn't have strong male role models in his life is the same symptoms of the Ahab spirit. Let's review; shall we; I know I am repeating myself but this is so important I need this implanted into your spirit. You don't want to fall prey to this spirit because this spirit presents as harmless but can do major damage to your purpose and destiny.

•A passive man

•Submitted to a controlling woman. (Often with women who has a title of Prophetess or Prophet)

•Feminized man

•Won't lead even in conversation he expects a woman to lead.

•Ahab doesn't speak up for his wife and children.

•Ahab is not a provider or protector. He can't give identity because he doesn't know his own identity. (Ahab is not a father figure)

•Compromising

•Quiet but not discerning

•No boundaries

•Intimidated by godly men. Doesn't have good male remodels or father figures to fill in the gap of his fatherlessness.

•Easily manipulated

•Doesn't speak up when wronged.

•Co-dependent (can't think for himself)

•A generational spirit (his father and grandfather are where Ahab's.)

•Didn't have good male role model's growing up, didn't have a strong father or father figure.

•Use to women taking care of him.

•Secretly suffers from anxiety, depression and chronic fear.

•Lacks leadership skills or the anointing of a leader but has a position or title of a leader.

•Is not discerning

•Doesn't like to be confronted with the truth, when he is confronted he will easily agree to avoid conflict but never changes his behavior because his heart doesn't change.

•Will easily put up with a controlling, manipulative woman.

•Expects a woman to take care of him.

•Is attracted to spiritual Jezebel's but not spiritual Esther's.

•Easily intimidated by a strong woman, while in a relationship with Jezebel (is secretly scared of her).

•May have a position, title or platform, but behind the scenes, Jezebel is running the show.

•Will sit at home sleeping while his woman works.

•Doesn't work or can't stay on a job for a long time.

•If single he goes from house to house with different women taking care of him.

•His mother was a Jezebel.

•His mother doesn't see a potential wife for her son as a potential daughter but rather someone to compete with. His mother took care of him much longer than she should have. He is an adult child.

•Came from a single parent household.

•Fear of confrontation.

•Fear of speaking the truth.

•Fear of rejection, insecure.

Beware, ladies, you can discern an Ahab when you don't really know him like that, but he starts disclosing past hurts, current complaints. He wants you to feel sorry for him, so you empathize so much that you start taking care of him. Ahab can't make decisions on his own or figure it out, so he starts talking to you.

•Ahab is passive aggressive. He can't say what he feels to you; he has to make sideways innuendos and comments. Ahab can't be assertive even if it is respectfully.

•Ahab is a grown man with the mentality of a little boy.

•Ahab if married will be the stay at home dad while his wife works. (which is out of order by God's standards by the way)

Why is this important?

Ahab is a passive spirit that fears confrontation. This is so important because many Christians don't want to speak for

God. They don't want to offend anyone. They want to sit in a corner and wait for Jesus to return. They don't want to evangelize the world of Jesus due to fear. Today's society wants us to be compromising Christians all in the name of love. If you read the life of Ahab, you would think he wasn't all that bad. He didn't do much wrong. Still, Ahab didn't do much right either. He wanted to turn a blind eye to what was going on in his own home with his controlling wife, Jezebel.

God didn't give Ahab a pass. Because Ahab never spoke up, God considered him evil because what he allowed to happen while he was a king. In fact, look what the scripture says about Ahab.

1 Kings 21:20-29Living Bible (TLB)

20 "So my enemy has found me!" Ahab exclaimed to Elijah.

"Yes," Elijah answered, "I have come to place God's curse upon you because you have sold yourself to the devil.[a]

21 The Lord is going to bring great harm to you and sweep you away; he will not let a single one of your male descendants survive!

22 He is going to destroy your family as he did the family of King Jeroboam and the family of King Baasha, for you have made him very angry and have led all of Israel into sin.

23 The Lord has also told me that the dogs of Jezreel shall tear apart the body of your wife, Jezebel.

24 The members of your family who die in the city shall be eaten by dogs, and those who die in the country shall be eaten by vultures."

25 No one else was so completely sold out to the devil as Ahab, for his wife, Jezebel, encouraged him to do every sort of evil.

26 He was especially guilty because he worshiped idols just as the Amorites did—the people whom the Lord had chased out of the land to make room for the people of Israel.

27 When Ahab heard these prophecies, he tore his clothing, put on rags, fasted, slept in sackcloth, and went about in deep humility.

28 Then another message came to Elijah:

29 "Do you see how Ahab has humbled himself before me? Because he has done this, I will not do what I promised during his lifetime; it will happen to his sons; I will destroy his descendants."

The thing about Ahab is that when confronted with his behavior, he is quick to humble himself and repent. His heart doesn't change, and neither did his behavior. Repent means to change. If you ask for forgiveness and don't change you are still doomed. Notice the prophetic declaration. My pastor told us the other day that even when a prophetic word is spoken it is your character that brings it to past. He said, "the prophetic word is based on the character that is consistent." In Ahab's case once he humbled himself before God, then God changes his mind not to destroy him.

Yet as stated Ahab's humble spirit didn't last long.

1 Kings 22:33-38Living Bible (TLB)

32-33 When they saw King Jehoshaphat in his royal robes, they thought, "That's the man we're after." So they wheeled around to attack him. But when Jehoshaphat shouted out to identify himself,[a] they turned back!

34 However, someone shot an arrow at random and it struck King Ahab between the joints of his armor.

"Take me out of the battle, for I am badly wounded," he groaned to his chariot driver.

35 The battle became more and more intense as the day wore on, and King Ahab went back in, propped up in his chariot with the blood from his wound running down onto the floorboards. Finally, toward evening, he died.

36-37 Just as the sun was going down the cry ran through his troops. "It's all over—return home! The king is dead!"

And his body was taken to Samaria and buried there.

38 When his chariot and armor were washed beside the pool of Samaria, where the prostitutes bathed, dogs came and licked the king's blood just as the Lord had said would happen.

Why is this important for us to learn about confidence?

Ahab is a passive spirit that submits to idolatry. Idolatry is idol worship. Ahab is afraid of confrontation. For us single ladies, although the Ahab spirit is present is both men and women we have to be careful not to date or marry a man who has the spirit of Ahab.

You can't walk in divine authority, and divine confidence with the spirit of Ahab attached to your life.

So how can Ahab get free?

We must acknowledge this Ahab spirit before God. God will not free you from what you don't acknowledge.

Endure the process. God will send Ahab's through a series of test to build their spiritual muscle and make them into the individual God has called them to be. The process is hard, gut-wrenching because through every step of the way Ahab is tempted to go back to Jezebel or go back to being taken care of because that is his unhealthy coping mechanism.

Do not! Do not! Go to being in a relationship. If Ahab is single, he must remain single until the processing is done. Any relationship including friendships, and romantic relationships will turn into an unhealthy codependent relationship because Ahab thrives on people taking care of him.

He needs someone "stronger" than himself to lean on. Ahab must learn to lean on God and must wait for God to release divine authority to him. Ahab must find his true identity. Anyone that Ahab finds himself in a relationship with he will take on their identity because he has no real sense of self. Ahab if your single, stay that way until God has done processing you. Ahab will force the person he is in a relationship with to lead because of his passive nature. They will eventually come to resent him because of this.

If you are married to an Ahab, it may be hard but stop pacifying Ahab. Hold him accountable. If he doesn't get it done don't do it for him. If Ahab refuses to work, you're going to have to show him tough love.

Ahab has big problems with boundaries, so you have to make your boundaries very clear. Boundaries must be both personally and professionally clear. Boundaries cannot be assumed they must be clearly and explicitly stated. You also have to check Ahab when he crosses those boundaries. And note Ahab will always cross boundaries even after they are clearly stated. You have to show Ahab you mean what you say.

Pray, pray, pray, endure the process then keep praying. This is important because we read that it is God's will to restore the father. If you have ever struggled with a passive spirit, you had an Ahab spirit. Passivity is really rooted in low confidence. We have to come into agreement with what God's will is when we pray so that heaven's agenda will manifest.

The Word, The Word, The Word. You must feed yourself the word of God to get free from the spirit of Ahab.

For scriptural reference see I Kings 18 and read your way through. Look for patterns in the relationship between Jezebel and Ahab.

Chapter 7

Jezebel Versus Esther

Esther 4:14(NKJV)

14 For if you remain completely silent at this time, relief and deliverance will arise for the Jews from another place, but you and your father's house will perish. Yet who knows whether you have come to the kingdom for such a time as this?"

The story of Esther is one of my favorite stories in the bible. Esther was an amazing woman. I can relate to her in so many ways. Esther started out the underdog. I am always rooting for the underdog. The underdog to me is the one least likely to succeed. The one everyone ignores, the one that people overlook. Believe it or not, God handpicks the underdog and chooses them as the one He will use to advance His kingdom. God doesn't look at the superstar to advance His kingdom. God doesn't see things as man does. Man looks at the outward appearance, but God looks at the heart. God doesn't choose the one that is most popular; He chooses the nerdy kid that no one likes. You know the secret of God's choosing because He tells us how He hands picks people in His word.

1 Samuel 16:7 (NKJV)

7 But the Lord said to Samuel, "Do not look at his appearance or at his physical stature, because I have refused him. For the

Lord does not see as man sees;[a] for man looks at the outward appearance, but the Lord looks at the heart."

1 Corinthians 1:27 (NKJV)

27 But God has chosen the foolish things of the world to put to shame the wise, and God has chosen the weak things of the world to put to shame the things which are mighty;

This is what leads us to the purpose of this chapter. In our previous chapter, we discussed the spirit of Ahab and his wicked wife, Jezebel. I want to make it clear that God uses us as women and men of God in positions of authority, and power. There is nothing wrong with that at all. I pray that we would have more unapologetically Christian leaders in different spheres of influence in our world, such as government, arts you name it. Unfortunately, we have many people in our world claiming Christ, but their lives don't match up. God wants to use His people to save humanity.

No there is nothing wrong with being a Christian politician, a Christian actor, a Christian motivational speaker, a Christian doctor, a Christian lawyer you name it. The problem comes in when we compromise. Unfortunately, I am increasingly aware of Christians who are seeking titles, prominence, and positions before God. It is almost as if God is an afterthought. We have raised a bunch of self-promoting, self-centered Christians. The world is dying, and we are worried about how many followers we have on social media. The lure of prominence has caused the body of Christ to be distracted from the real motive for ministry. It is like the body of Christ doesn't really have the heart for God, but they claim Him, to use Him to advance their self-centered agenda. In fact, here is a quote that I posted on Facebook the other day.

Unfortunately, we have created a generation of self-seeking, self-motivated saints thereby leaving us with a body of believers who are social media savvy but powerless to advancing heavens agenda.

People are dying, and the Christians are worried about how many likes or dislikes they get on social media. Why does it matter? Better yet who cares?

While the world is lost. Many Christians could care less. We want to talk about ourselves, our ministries, our agendas, our successes, our latest and greatest whatever. Much of it may be beneficial to a certain extent but has no real kingdom value.

Jesus came to seek that which is lost. Does it save the lost? Heal the sick? (Emotionally, mentally, spiritually, and physically). Does it promote the agenda of Christ FIRST not as an afterthought to solidify our false motives? Can you cast out a demon? Did you give yourself that title? Does it promote your own glory at the end of the day? Are you seeking God and all His righteousness and these (material) things be added? Or are we seeking material things, trying to use Christ to use His name to falsely promote your stuff? Are living holy? Be honest with yourself.

But God.....

There is a remnant that has not fallen prey to the idol of materialism that God is calling forth. It won't be who you think and certainly not many of these self-promotors who claim God's will, but their hearts are far from Him.

Therefore, God chose the underdog. He doesn't want to use, self-promotion, self-centered, seeking their own glory individual. God chooses the underdog because the underdog isn't seeking to be promoted or honored in the first place.

That leads us to discuss the difference between Esther versus Jezebel. There are many examples of God choosing the underdog in scripture. The story of Esther is just one of many. Nevertheless, it is important to note that most underdogs have the same character flaw in the beginning, and that is they struggle with their confidence. Moses reminded God of his stuttering problem, David was rejected by his brothers and his biological father, Isaiah told God how unclean he was. Then that leads us to Esther. Esther was a quiet girl, whose parents had died when she was a kid, she was a foreigner in the land, she was raised by her Uncle Mordecai. Esther applied for the position of Queen in obedience to her Uncle. She was very respectful and submitted to those who God had put over her. She just so happened by God's divine plan to be selected for the position. When you are the underdog, God's favor puts you in positions that others self-promotion, marketing strategies, and plans could never put them in. Then Esther is by the hand of God and to her surprise is put in a position over a nation of people. To add to it, she ends up being put in the position of having to save a nation. She could die, she had to be convinced by her uncle to do something.

Her heart was in no way trying to seek prominence, but God positioned her for it. She responded with obedience. That leads us to the scripture which was a conversation between

Esther and Mordecai. He had to tell her to step up. She responded by saying, "I will, and if I die I die."

Esther 4:11-17Living Bible (TLB)

11 "All the world knows that anyone, whether man or woman, who goes into the king's inner court without his summons is doomed to die unless the king holds out his gold scepter; and the king has not called for me to come to him in more than a month."

12 So Hathach gave Esther's message to Mordecai.

13 This was Mordecai's reply to Esther: "Do you think you will escape there in the palace when all other Jews are killed?

14 If you keep quiet at a time like this, God will deliver the Jews from some other source, but you and your relatives will die; what's more, who can say but that God has brought you into the palace for just such a time as this?"

15 Then Esther sent this message to Mordecai:

16 "Go and gather together all the Jews of Shushan and fast for me; do not eat or drink for three days, night or day; and I and my maids will do the same; and then, though it is strictly forbidden, I will go in to see the king; and if I perish, I perish."

17 So Mordecai did as Esther told him to.

We will study more about the relationship between Jezebel and her Uncle Mordecai in another chapter.

I just love Esther. Then there was Jezebel. Jezebel was an entirely different person entirely. She was a self-seeking, perverted woman. She wanted prominence and position at all cost. She wanted it so much she would kill and destroy an entire nation to get what she wanted. Before we move on, we must understand the difference between the spirit of Jezebel versus the virtue of Esther.

As stated Esther is not a spirit, the spirit that she walked in was the spirit of God. She displayed characteristics a God-fearing woman. To truly understand the spirit that she walked in we must understand Proverbs 31, which is about a virtuous woman. Virtuous means purity of heart, mind, and spirit.

Virtuous means moral character, moral excellence and a righteous heart before God and others with whom she interacts with. If we are going to understand Esther's spirit, we must consider and understand Proverbs 31. Again, if we identify at least five characteristics, we know that this individual encompasses the spirit of Esther, otherwise known as a virtuous woman.

We must understand that God wants us to be in positions of power, authority and influence. Yet, He still wants our heart to be towards him. Just because someone has authority, power and influence doesn't mean that they have a heart for God or that God is the one who has elevated them. That brings us study the differences between Queen Jezebel versus Queen Esther.

As stated it is a demonic agenda sent by satan himself to emasculate the man. Emasculate means deprive (a man) of his male role or identity. We see this subtle demonic attack in our world in a greater way. Unfortunately, many Christians have fallen prey to the demonic agenda because we have to many Christians who are carnal, fleshly driven. Whenever an individual is carnally driven, they cannot see or perceive the things of the spirit. They certainly cannot see the plan or agenda of the enemy, because his deception is based up the spirit of delusion and deception. Just because it looks right, doesn't mean it is right.

The demonic agenda that is infiltering our world is coming in the form of the feminist agenda. The feminist agenda appears to be about fighting for women's rights, and equality. Sounds great right? Well if you study further and look at the principles of the perspective it really is based on the spirit of Jezebel. Don't get me wrong I am not against a woman being in positions of power and authority. I am a woman who is very much empowered in ministry, entrepreneurship, and life. We cannot deny the demonic agenda of satan.

God wants and expects women to operate in power, authority, dominion, in ministry, business, and in every area of our lives. Yet, he never created us to be in competition with a man. He never created us to emasculate them so that we can be in charge.

This is why I write this chapter. There is difference between the spirit of Jezebel (feminist agenda) versus a woman who walks in authority designated by the spirit of God..

For us to get clarity, we must understand the difference between the Jezebel Spirit (Queen Jezebel) versus Queen Esther (Proverbs 31). This chapter proves that a woman can be in a position of power, authority, kingdom minded while being covered, ordained and sent from God. We must know the difference, so we are aware of the differences in the demonic agenda versus the kingdom of God agenda.

Similarities

•Both were married to Kings. Esther was married to King Ahasuerus. Jezebel was married to King Ahab.

•Both had positions of power and authority

•Both had the kings heart.

•Both were beautiful

•Both were leaders

•Both were prophetic

•Both had the power to make decisions

•Both had power and influence

•Both were very intelligent

Differences

•Jezebel almost destroyed a nation. Esther saved a nation.

•Jezebel sought power by any means necessary. Esther never sought power but was put in a position of power by God.

Esther 4:14 (KJV)

14 For if thou altogether holdest thy peace at this time, then shall there enlargement and deliverance arise to the Jews from another place; but thou and thy father's house shall be destroyed: and who knoweth whether thou art come to the kingdom for such a time as this?

•Jezebel was controlling and manipulative.

•Esther was the complete opposite not controlling, not manipulative, quiet, discerning and kind.

•Esther was honored by God. God despised Jezebel because of her actions.

•Esther was submitted to her leaders including her adoptive father, and husband.

•Jezebel was unsubmitted, she usurped (to take, seize, disregard) her husband's authority for her own agenda.

•Esther respected her husband's authority, and didn't have her own agenda, but had an agenda for God's kingdom to be saved.

•Jezebel served false idols (Baal)

•Esther served God.

•Jezebel never sought counsel from others. She only sought other false prophets who would help to advance her demonic agenda.

•Esther sought wise counsel from godly fatherly leaders such as her Uncle Mordecai who was a godly man who honored God with his life.

•Jezebel father was an idol worshiper.

There is so much more that we can say about their difference. My point is God never made any assumptions that women can't be powerful, in positions of authority, and influence. If we are going to be women who advance God's kingdom, if we are to be used powerfully to save our nation and our world, we must renounce this feminist agenda (Jezebel's agenda really) and embrace Esther's spirit (spirit of the

Proverbs 31 woman). Again God wants us to be powerful beyond belief. He doesn't want us to play politics, disrespect the authority of a man, or leaders, be manipulative or controlling for our own agenda. The remainder of the chapter is how to identify the agenda/spirit of Jezebel versus and how to identify the agenda/spirit of Esther. If you want to be honored by God, we must see through the eyes of Esther.

Identifying the Jezebel spirit in others:

Note you don't have to have all identified, but if you identify at least of five the traits noted, we know that you struggle with a spirit of Jezebel. Note the Jezebel spirit can be found in both men and women.

•Embraces false god's, goddesses, African spiritualist, ancient beliefs, tarot cards, psychic mediums, light work.

•Is spiritual but doesn't identify herself as a Christian. Or if she does identify herself as a Christian she still embraces other spiritual beliefs that are outside of the realm of Christ.

•Difficulty in relationships with men.

•May have been married multiple times.

•Difficulty submitting.

•Calls herself a prophet, a prophetess. If she isn't embraced or put in a leadership position in the church, she will leave start her own church and give herself a title of prophet, prophetess, apostle and or bishop.

•Controlling

•Manipulative

•Unsubmitted

•Plays psychological games to get you or her husband to give her what she wants. She can cry fake tears at the drop of a dime.

•Sexually perverted.

•Embraces LGBT movement.

•Jezebel secretly suffers from church hurt; she was rejected by the church whether it was warranted or not. Because she is secretly hurting whenever something happens in our world whether it be a natural disaster, political unrest, crime, scandal she uses use Facebook and social media as a means to subtly, attack the church, Christians, Christian leaders and its members.

•Because of her leadership capability, she is often put in positions of leadership within the church.

•Starts her own church and slowly begins to put seeds of discord in the hearts of others towards their leaders with the agenda of getting people to embrace her and her movement.

•Her ministry is not about advancing the kingdom of God; but has a hidden motive highlighting her and her own importance.

•Calls herself a "spiritual father" to others. Contrary to popular belief a spiritual mother is NOT the same as a spiritual father but both of them have their place within the kingdom of God. A woman is NOT a spiritual Father, NEITHER is a man a spiritual mother. These are two separate but needed positions of authority within the body of Christ. A woman cannot be a spiritual father. A man cannot be spiritual mother. We will study more about this in another chapter.

•Has blatant disregard for the rights of others.

•Secretly jealous and envious of others position of authority particular of another man's authority.

•Always has a false agenda. She can't do something out of the kindness of her heart; she does something with the expectation of getting something in return.

•Will use tears as a means or manipulation.

•Co-dependent. Jezebel needs someone with the spirit of Ahab for her to be successful. This is why we have this demonic agenda to emasculate the man. Jezebel has to dethrone Ahab's position for her to push her demonic agenda.

•Secretly envious of other women. (intimidated but she is not going to tell you and will display the opposite.)

•Anytime a woman constantly has other conflicts with other women Jezebel's spirit is in the midst somewhere.

•Insecure

•Spiritual but not Christian.

•Flesh driven.

•Prideful, arrogant, conceded

•Want to be on top at all cost.

•Sexually provocative.

•Doesn't have a true father, father figure. If she does, he is more than likely another Ahab.

•Is married to a man with a position but she is really running the show. (Pastor, co-pastor, etc.)

•Wants to be needed and will create chaos in others in order to be needed.

•Controlling of her grown children.

•Prophetic is often known for her prophetic accuracy and is put in a position of authority within the church. Just because someone is prophetic doesn't mean God sent them. Jezebel's prophetic accuracy came from the demonic spirit of Baal.

•Has been diagnosed with borderline personality disorder.

•If Jezebel and Esther lived around the same time. Jezebel would hate Esther because she represents everything she is not. Esther has more power than Jezebel. To Jezebel Esther represents power and position without having to be evil and manipulative to get it.

•When you walk in the spirit of Esther (a proverbs 31 woman) you will be hated by those who have the Jezebel spirit.

Discerning the Spirit of Esther A Virtuous God Fearing, God Anointed Woman.

Proverbs 31:10-31 Living Bible (TLB)

10 If you can find a truly good wife, she is worth more than precious gems!

11 Her husband can trust her, and she will richly satisfy his needs. (married, but also can be single, trust worthy)

12 She will not hinder him but help him all her life. (helper)

13 She finds wool and flax and busily spins it. (resourceful)

14 She buys imported foods brought by ship from distant ports. (entrepreneurial mind)

15 She gets up before dawn to prepare breakfast for her household and plans the day's work for her servant girls. (diligent)

16 She goes out to inspect a field and buys it; with her own hands she plants a vineyard. (property owner)

17 She is energetic, a hard worker,

18 and watches for bargains. She works far into the night! (spends money wisely)

19-20 She sews for the poor and generously helps those in need. (giving heart)

21 She has no fear of winter for her household, for she has made warm clothes for all of them. (no anxiety or worries)

22 She also upholsters with finest tapestry; her own clothing is beautifully made—a purple gown of pure linen. (knows how to dress)

23 Her husband is well known, for he sits in the council chamber with the other civic leaders. (is wise about the type of man she marries, they compliment each other)

24 She makes belted linen garments to sell to the merchants. (entrepreneur)

25 She is a woman of strength and dignity and has no fear of old age. (the heart of God)

26 When she speaks, her words are wise, and kindness is the rule for everything she says. (wisdom)

27 She watches carefully all that goes on throughout her household and is never lazy.

28 Her children stand and bless her; so does her husband. He praises her with these words:

29 "There are many fine women in the world, but you are the best of them all!"

30 Charm can be deceptive and beauty doesn't last, but a woman who fears and reverences God shall be greatly praised.

31 Praise her for the many fine things she does. These good deeds of hers shall bring her honor and recognition from people of importance.[a]

So she was a powerful woman, but she had the heart for and from God. She is the complete opposite of the spirit of Jezebel. Let us consider some other characteristics of Esther.

Esther's Spirit

•Willing to seek out godly counsel from others.

•Has fatherly godly influence.

•Submitted to leaders that God has placed before her.

•Kind

•Caring

•Nurturing

•Exhibits strength and honor.

- Honors her husband doesn't try to overrule his authority.

- Is not self-seeking or self-serving

- Humility

- Humility

- Humility

- Respectful

- Modest

- Submits to God and His authority

- Advances God's agenda not her own.

- Doesn't give herself a title.

- Waits to be honored.

- Waits for divine instructions.

- A righteous heart

- Confident

- Has standards, won't compromise them in order to gain success

- Understands who she is in God.

- Successful by her own means, is not co-dependent. She has been favored by God.

- Because her heart is pure before God, God Himself appoints her to positions of power and authority. She never has to disrespect anyone in the process of elevation. Great reputation.

There is so much more that we can say about this topic. I encourage you to continue study read I Kings 18 and go on through to see Jezebel and her reign, then read the book of Esther. Compare and contrast what you see. Remember Esther was honored by God, her husband, and a nation. While Jezebel dishonored God, dishonored her husband, who also dishonored God and dishonored a nation.

Again, it is not that women can't be in positions of power, authority and dominion we must go about it God's way and not the way of Jezebel.

This is so important for us as men and women of God. We must know that we have been chosen to advance God's kingdom for such a time as this. Still, many people who secretly suffer with low self-worth and value seek prominence so that they can be validated by people. They seek positions to stroke their egos and help them to feel as if they are going to be okay. We must check our motives at the door. The minute your motive for success is to gain acceptance from people you are no longer fit to be used for the kingdom.

Moses wasn't able to make it to the promise land because he took his eyes off of God and put it on the opinions

of man.

John 12:42-43 (NKJV)

42 Nevertheless even among the rulers many believed in Him, but because of the Pharisees they did not confess Him, lest they should be put out of the synagogue;

43 for they loved the praise of men more than the praise of God.

When you walk in God confidence you love God more than the praise of people. Your confidence is not based upon who likes you and who doesn't. We talked earlier about the spirit of rejection, when a person is motivated by self-gain the underlying issue is rejection. Remember we are called to serve.

So how we grow in confidence? We have to check our motives for seeking success. Confidence grows as you work in and on your purpose, still somewhere along the way, if our motives are not pure, pursuit of purpose becomes pursuit of prominence, pursuit of accolades from people, or pursuit of validation.

Part III: The Antidote

Chapter 8

Sonship

Galatians 4:7 (TLB)

7 Now we are no longer slaves but God's own sons. And since we are his sons, everything he has belongs to us, for that is the way God planned.

Once we understand the principles of sonship, it will greatly impact how we see ourselves and how we see God. Understand that we belong to God, this knowing is not only powerful but enduring. Knowing that you are a king's kid puts you at a greater advantage to being successful and to walk in the power of God. I want you to read through this chapter slowly. Don't rush it. We will talk about what sonship is. Yet we will also have to explore how sonship becomes perverted. We must have a true understanding of what sonship is and what sonship is not.

Many have come along and damaged those in the body of Christ all in the name of sonship, yet, their actions, words, and needs had nothing to do with sonship. It had everything to do with egos and demonic agendas. It may not make sense right now but go with me it will make sense in a minute.

First, let us review the past the role that father's play in the lives of their children. We said that the role of the father was to provide, protect and to give identity. We also talked about what happens when a father is not a part of our upbringing. We identified the term to be spiritual Ahab's.

The antidote (answer) and the problem is found in sonship. It sounds confusing I know but go with. Sonship found the right way delivers you from all insecurity, all fear, and allows you to walk in divine confidence. Sonship that is perverted puts you on the path to spiritual suicide. Perverted sonship left unchecked will cost you everything including your destiny. We need sonship in our lives, but we have to be aware of the pitfalls of perverted sonship, so we can avoid being deceived or falling prey to perverted sonship.

First, let us begin by discussing what a son is. I know everybody knows what a son is, but go with me. There is a reason why we must discuss this. What is a son? A son is a male who is a direct relative of his father. A son is a blood relative, a man or boy closely associated with or thought of as a child of something (as a country, race, or religion). What about a daughter what is a daughter? A daughter is a female offspring; a girl or woman about her parents. 2. a female descendant. 3. a female from a certain country.

Before we go forward for the sake of the text, we will use the word son to indicate sonship. Though, it is noted that according to scripture we are using this term to mean a son or a daughter, both have the same meaning. In the eyes of Jesus through grace one is not better than the other, we are all one in Christ Jesus.

Galatians 3:27-29 (KJV)

27 For as many of you as have been baptized into Christ have put on Christ.

28 There is neither Jew nor Greek, there is neither bond nor free, there is neither male nor female: for ye are all one in Christ Jesus.

29 And if ye be Christ's, then are ye Abraham's seed, and heirs according to the promise.

What are the roles of a son or daughter? Think about it.

In my work as a counselor we are taught what is called family systems theory. According to family systems theory we don't operate in isolation from one another but each individual within the family has a certain role, responsibility and unique positioning within the home. The problem comes in when our families are not healthy, and we grow up in dysfunction, that is when we define the family as a dysfunctional family.

Within each family different people have a different task, fathers provide, protect, and give identity. Mothers console, comfort, give wisdom and good counsel. Go with me.

So what do you think the role of the child is as it relates to their upbringing?

 Children may have home responsibilities as cleaning their rooms, studying getting good grades, those are the day to day task. But, the greater responsibility that parents expect of their children it to become capable adults, successful and to be productive citizens. Ultimately every parent wants their children to do better, live better and be more successful than they were. Every parent wants their children to not follow in the same footsteps that they did. Ultimately parents want their children to carry on the family name. In fact, the Bible clearly spells out one major responsibility of the children, to bring honor and to obey.

Deuteronomy 5:16 (NKJV)

16 'Honor your father and your mother, as the Lord your God has commanded you, that your days may be long, and that it may be well with you in the land which the Lord your God is giving you.

Ephesians 6:1-3 (NKJV)

1 Children, obey your parents in the Lord, for this is right.

 2 "Honor your father and mother," which is the first commandment with promise:

3 "that it may be well with you and you may live long on the earth."[a]

You can't disrespect your parents and think you will have success and long life. It doesn't matter the condition in which you were raised; your parents still deserve to be honored according to scripture. Notice the scripture didn't say if they treat you right. That doesn't mean you allow yourself to be abused. I have many clients's I work with that may have been neglected or abandoned by their parents. Some can't have a relationship with them because their parents are very unhealthy. Yet, there is a way to respectfully set boundaries. You can honor someone without having a relationship with them particularly if they are abusive. My mother was not raised by her biological mother; she was raised by her grandparents. Her father abandoned her at birth, she never met him. My mother never allowed bitterness or unforgiveness towards either parent. She had been nothing but a Christian to my grandmother, up until her death. My grandmother, my mother's mother had a severe mental illness and a drinking problem. My mother treated her with kindness and when she died my grandmother was saved because of my mother's testimony.

What if my mother wasn't a Christian. What if she allowed the hurt to make her bitter? I have had clients who curse their parents out and want nothing to do with them. That is sad. Even though my mother had reason to be bitter and unforgiving, she chose not to be.

A few months ago, I was on my way home and stopped at the gas station to fill up. There I listened in horror. I saw a young girl who looked to be about 19; it appeared to be her mother in the car. There she was screaming, hollering, and cussing her mother out. The words I heard I would never listen to let repeat. I was in shock; she was so loud that other people at the gas station took notice. The mother just sat in the car, quiet, not saying anything but smoking a cigarette. I thought to myself it doesn't matter what your mother did or didn't do in your life, no one deserves to be treated like that.

The way the mother had no expression, no reaction, no sense of awe or shock I could tell this behavior from her daughter was not a one-time incident, but something that had happened many times before.

My point is it shameful when we dishonor our parents. Why because there is an expectation that we will honor the family name. Trust me this is going to come together in a minute. What about those who don't have a father or a mother? What do we call someone who has been abandoned by their parents? We call them orphans. An orphan is someone whose parents are dead or have been abandoned by their parents. Now let's take it to the spiritual aspect.

What happens when we have had natural parents, but they mistreated us, used us and abused us? What happens when you feel as if you don't belong? What we then take on is mother and father wounds. We also take on what is called an orphan spirit. Mother and father wounds are emotional wounds that come because of an emotionally, mentally, and or spiritually absent mother or father.

In all of that if we want to get back to our identity in God we must embrace sonship. Let's go back to the primary function of the father. The primary function of the father is to provide, protect and to give identity. If we are going to walk in divine confidence the father must give us our identity, we have to be confident in His divine protection and that He will provide. A few weeks ago, I was working with a client who suffered from severe anxiety. I prayed as asked God what direction to take with her. He responded when an individual is affirmed in the love of the Father it cast out fear. Fear is anxiety. I knew that in our counseling session we would have to review and discuss how she sees the Father's love.

My point is the Bible gives us a clear indication of how we can cast out fear and walk in divine confidence.

As stated we must be affirmed, confidence, and self-assured in the Father's love towards us.

1 John 4:18 (KJV)

18 There is no fear in love; but perfect love casteth out fear: because fear hath torment. He that feareth is not made perfect in love.

We must understand that Father God is a good Father and He not only loves us, but He cares for us. I had a dream recently where a child was in danger. The father almost died trying to save his child. I heard the father say, "I would do it again because I love them." My point is God was showing me the love of a father ." Think about the ultimate sacrifice that God did for us. He showed us the perfect love of a father. Let's us look at some other scriptures that showed us His love displayed in words and in action.

John 3:16 (KJV)

16 For God so loved the world, that he gave his only begotten Son, that whosoever believeth in him should not perish, but have everlasting life.

What do real fathers do? They give unselfishly of themselves for their children. What motivated God to give His only son? It was love.

In our society, we don't have the same value in the father role because there an epidemic of children growing up in fatherless homes. The truth is that a real father is not selfish he gives. Imagine a father knowing that their child is hungry goes out and spends his last bit of money on an outfit or a new video game. We would call that a selfish father. God is not like that. His love is real; God gave His only son because He loved us. Loved motivated God, nothing more. When we know and understand the depth of the love God has for us we won't be so quick to doubt it. When we doubt God we secretly doubt His love towards us.

Matthew 7:11 (NKJV)

11 If you then, being evil, know how to give good gifts to your children, how much more will your Father who is in heaven give good things to those who ask Him!

James 1:17-18 (NKJV)

17 Every good gift and every perfect gift is from above, and comes down from the Father of lights, with whom there is no variation or shadow of turning.

18 Of His own will He brought us forth by the word of truth, that we might be a kind of first fruits of His creature.

Because God is a good father, He doesn't always give us what we want when we want it. He does give us His inheritance after He has developed us into who He has ordained and prepared for us to be. Think about when a baby comes into the world a good father doesn't just send them out into the world; they prepare you, train you and develop you so that you can be who he has prepared for you to be.

Galatians 4:1-2 (NKJV)

4 Now I say that the heir, as long as he is a child, does not differ at all from a slave, though he is master of all,

2 but is under guardians and stewards until the time appointed by the father.

Luke 12:32 (NKJV)

32 "Do not fear, little flock, for it is your Father's good pleasure to give you the kingdom.

Hopefully, I am painting a good picture of the father's love. To bring it home let's read a few more scriptures about the father's love.

Psalm 103:13 (NKJV)

13 As a father pities his children,

So the Lord pities those who fear Him.

When the scriptures say, the word fear it means to reverence, show in high regard, to honor. God doesn't want us to be afraid of Him like any worthy father, He wants us to honor and respect Him.

Romans 5:8 (NKJV)

8 But God demonstrates His own love toward us, in that while we were still sinners, Christ died for us.

John 15:13-15 New King James Version (NKJV)

13 Greater love has no one than this, than to lay down one's life for his friends.

14 You are My friends if you do whatever I command you.

15 No longer do I call you servants, for a servant does not know what his master is doing; but I have called you friends, for all things that I heard from My Father I have made known to you.

Maybe you can't say that your father is your best friend, maybe there are those of you who can. Whatever your situation God can be your best friend.

Proverbs 13:24 (NKJV)

24 He who spares his rod hates his son,

But he who loves him disciplines him promptly.

God in His love disciplines us. Funny story when I was a little kid, I asked my father did God ever spank his children. My dad responded yes. I remember being afraid of God because I kept thinking of how much a spanking hurt and that I wouldn't want to get a spanking from God. My dad didn't explain that too well for me. My father was trying to explain to me that God disciplines us, but he didn't tell me that God doesn't come down from heaven and spank us. Talk about the fear of the Lord.

Hebrews 12:6-11 (NKJV)

6 For whom the Lord loves He chastens,

And scourges every son whom He receives."[a]

7 If[b] you endure chastening, God deals with you as with sons; for what son is there whom a father does not chasten?

8 But if you are without chastening, of which all have become partakers, then you are illegitimate and not sons.

9 Furthermore, we have had human fathers who corrected us, and we paid them respect. Shall we not much more readily be in subjection to the Father of spirits and live?

10 For they indeed for a few days chastened us as seemed best to them, but He for our profit, that we may be partakers of His holiness.

11 Now no chastening seems to be joyful for the present, but painful; nevertheless, afterward it yields the peaceable fruit of righteousness to those who have been trained by it.

Chasten means to discipline or punish. It also means to inflict suffering upon for purposes of moral improvement; chastise. I know some of you believe that God will never punish you because of the grace message. Nevertheless, you would be wrong, it is right here in the world of God, in the new testament and still under the new and old covenant. God doesn't take pleasure in punishing us, but like any good father, he punishes us to make us better.

A father that doesn't ever discipline their child is a neglectful father no matter how much they love their children.

God is not nor, has he ever been a neglectful father.

We must continue our discussion. We must understand how to be good son and daughters to be able to embrace God's love. What happens when you don't have that example of a father in your life? At times it can be difficult to understand the love of the father when you have never seen it displayed in your life.

Yet as stated if we are going to walk in divine confidence we must understand what the father means to us? Before we move on to part II of this chapter, I want you see the words of one of my favorite by songwriters Chris Tomlin, Good Good Father.

Good Good Father

Chris Tomlin

I've heard a thousand stories of what they think you're like

But I've heard the tender whispers of love in the dead of night

And you tell me that you're pleased

And that I'm never alone

You're a good father

It's who you are; it's who you are, it's who you are

And I'm loved by you

It's who I am; it's who I am, it's who I am

I've seen many searching for answers far and wide

But I know we're all searching

For answers only you provide

'Cause you know just what we need

Before we say a word

You're a good good father

It's who you are, it's who you are, it's who you are

And I'm loved by you

It's who I am, it's who I am, it's who I am

Because you are perfect in all of your ways

You are perfect in all of your ways

You are perfect in all of your ways to us

You are…

A Good Father (2015) as found at; https://www.azlyrics.com/lyrics/christomlin/goodgoodfather.html cited on: January 29, 2018

It is true once you begin to seek the love you have been missing in Father God. He will fulfill you. He will tell you who you are, He will wipe your tears, He will sing over you with His love. He will hug you, laugh with you and make you feel safe in a way your earthly father could never. Father God will fulfill your need for a father.

Psalm 27:10 (NKJV)

10 When my father and my mother forsake me,

Then the Lord will take care of me.

Zephaniah 3:17 (NKJV)

17 The Lord your God in your midst,

The Mighty One, will save;

He will rejoice over you with gladness,

He will quiet you with His love,

He will rejoice over you with singing."

Imagine your father cheering you on, singing over you while your sleep. His eyes big, His smile wide and all He can think about is how He is consumed with how much He loves you. In deed He is a good father. He is seeking you, you must also respond to Him. Don't keep Him waiting, Father God wants to commune, talk with you and tell you who you really are.

Jeremiah 29:11-13 (NKJV)

11 For I know the thoughts that I think toward you, says the Lord, thoughts of peace and not of evil, to give you a future and a hope.

12 Then you will call upon Me and go and pray to Me, and I will listen to you.

13 And you will seek Me and find Me, when you search for Me with all your heart.

Chapter 9

Sonship

Part II

Romans 8:15 (NKJV)

15 For you did not receive the spirit of bondage again to fear, but you received the Spirit of adoption by whom we cry out, "Abba, Father."

We have all been adopted. Yes, that's right adopted. I received a call from a young lady a few years back she wanted to schedule a counseling. When we discussed further her purpose for seeking counseling session, she reported that she was struggling with feeling abandoned and not wanted because she had been adopted. She felt the abandonment from her birth parents even though her adoptive parents had chosen her.

This feeling of abandonment is not uncommon for individuals who have been adopted. Even if they have never met their birth parents, there is this underlying thought that focuses on being let go of by their birth parents. I still want you to hold on to the fact that you have been adopted. We all have been adopted. We must declare this thought as a badge of honor. First, let's explored what it means to be adopted. Adopted means to choose or take as one's own; make one's own by selection or assent. To take and rear (the child of other parents) as one's child, specifically by a formal legal action, to take or receive into any new relationship, to adopt a person as a protégé to select, accept.

When you have been adopted, you have been specifically selected, chosen. Look at the scripture we read at the beginning of the chapter.

Romans 8:15 (TLB)

15 And so we should not be like cringing, fearful slaves, but we should behave like God's very own children, adopted into the bosom of his family, and calling to him, "Father, Father."

Psalm 27:10 (TLB)

10 For if my father and mother should abandon me, you would welcome and comfort me.

So, when you look at it from that perspective adoption is not a bad thing it is a good thing. Many look at adoption from the negative connotation. We talked about the role of the father in our last chapter, but I want you to see how God adopts us. The wonderful thing about it is something supernatural happens when we embrace the father's adoption.

Romans 11:17 (TLB)

17 But some of these branches from Abraham's tree, some of the Jews, have been broken off. And you Gentiles who were branches from, we might say, a wild olive tree, were grafted in. So now you, too, receive the blessing God has promised

Abraham and his children, sharing in God's rich nourishment of his special olive tree.

Graft means to join by such union; it means to be molded into.

When God adopts you, you are not the outcast; you are not the adopted child, you are His. The more you grow in Him and continue in your relationship with Him, you begin to take on His nature, you then take on His DNA, you have His blood type. This is something that doesn't happen with natural, adopted children. Yes, you may look like them, you may even start sounding like your adoptive parents because the more you spend time with someone in a relationship you begin to take on each other characteristics. Still, if you have the opposite blood type, it will never change. You will never have their DNA, not so with God.

My point is if we are going to walk as a royal child of God we must embrace His adoption. We must submit to the process of sonship.

1 Peter 2:9 Living Bible (TLB)

9 But you are not like that, for you have been chosen by God himself—you are priests of the King, you are holy and pure, you are God's very own—all this so that you may show to others how God called you out of the darkness into his wonderful light.

1 Peter 2:9 King James Version (KJV)

9 But ye are a chosen generation, a royal priesthood, an holy nation, a peculiar people; that ye should shew forth the

praises of him who hath called you out of darkness into his marvellous light;

Ever felt stranger, like you were the odd one out like you didn't fit? Well get encouraged you are in good company. Your Abba created you that way.

Ever been rejected, overlooked, ignored, be confident your Abba Father made you that way for a reason.

Peculiar means stranger, odd, weird, unusual. I saw a move the other day and one of the main characters said to another, "don't try to fit in when you were created to stand out."

1 Corinthians 1:27-30 Living Bible (TLB)

27 Instead, God has deliberately chosen to use ideas the world considers foolish and of little worth in order to shame those people considered by the world as wise and great.

28 He has chosen a plan despised by the world, counted as nothing at all, and used it to bring down to nothing those the world considers great,

29 so that no one anywhere can ever brag in the presence of God.

30 For it is from God alone that you have your life through Christ Jesus. He showed us God's plan of salvation; he was the one who made us acceptable to God; he made us pure and holy[a] and gave himself to purchase our salvation.

Maybe, just maybe your rejection, your being abandoned was a divine set up from God? Think about it.

Nevertheless, we have to understand sonship? What is it? There are times when God will send us spiritual leaders who also embrace us as father. Most of us refer to them as spiritual fathers. People who have an apostolic grace upon their life often have spiritual children. It means children that are not related to them by blood, but they are discipled and are fathered advance God's kingdom. The Apostle Paul would often refer to his spiritual sons as his son, although he had no birth children of his own. Timothy was a great example of this. A mentor is not the same thing as a father. A mentor is someone who simply gives you advice, but a spiritual father is someone who does so much more. A spiritual father is concerned about birthing your destiny.

2 Timothy 1:2 (TLB)

2 To: Timothy, my dear son. May God the Father and Christ Jesus our Lord shower you with his kindness, mercy, and peace.

There is nothing wrong with a spiritual father or a spiritual son as long as they are leading you to a closer relationship with God. God will at times give us spiritual parents to help develop the call of God on our lives.

Let's consider this more thoroughly. There are many examples in the bible, the relationship between Moses and Joshua is one among many.

Moses and Joshua were not related by blood. Joshua's biological father's name was Nun. Moses acted as a father and gave him a new identity, which meant giving him a new name.

Numbers 13:16 (NKJV)

16 These are the names of the men whom Moses sent to spy out the land. And Moses called Hoshea[a] the son of Nun, Joshua

Just because you have a biological father present in your life doesn't mean that God won't give you a spiritual father.

Something that is very important in the relationship between a father and a son is that a true father always desires to pass something on to the son. Sometimes it is the birth of a ministry; the family busines, sometimes it is their spirit, sometimes the son is their replacement. It is very important to note that a true spiritual father wants you to be more successful than they are, they want you to complete the assignment. Remember we already discussed early the role of parents. The role of spiritual parents are very similar. A spiritual father always leaves you an inheritance, it doesn't always have to be a physical monetary inheritance, but they do leave you with something.

Deuteronomy 34:9 (NKJV)

9 Now Joshua the son of Nun was full of the spirit of wisdom, for Moses had laid his hands on him; so the children of Israel heeded him, and did as the Lord had commanded Moses.

Proverbs 13:22 (KJV)

22 A good man leaveth an inheritance to his children's children: and the wealth of the sinner is laid up for the just.

Inheritance is the practice of passing on property, titles, debts, rights, and obligations upon the death of an individual.

Inheritance means to pass down to another generation or generations.

Before we go forward let's talk about the role of the son (daughter). There are many examples in the word of God. Still, I want to highlight one for the ladies. Often when we think of spiritual sons, we think of a father and son, we don't think of a daughter and father.

By the way, to reiterate a woman can only be a spiritual mother, a father can only be a spiritual father. A woman can't be a spiritual father, neither can a father be a spiritual mother. Only God can be both mother and father.

Let's look at an example of sonship between a spiritual father and a daughter. Note this text is quite long so I will not sit here and have you read the entire biblical story but will highlight a few points. The text is so good; I highly recommend that you read the text on your own time. Ready let's go.

Esther 2:7-8 (NKJV)

7 And Mordecai had brought up Hadassah, that is, Esther, his uncle's daughter, for she had neither father nor mother. The young woman was lovely and beautiful. **When her father and mother died, Mordecai took her as his own daughter.**

8 So it was, when the king's command and decree were heard, and when many young women were gathered at Shushan the citadel, under the custody of Hegai, that Esther also was taken to the king's palace, into the care of Hegai the custodian of the women.

Do you see the correlation from what we already learned? First Esther was an orphan. Her uncle became her father. The story of Esther is what we call typology. Typology is the study and interpretation of types and symbols, originally especially in the Bible.

It simply means we look at this true story to consider the greater meaning and how the story reflects our relationship with God.

Mordecai represents the love of a father, the spirit of adoption. Esther represents us, abandoned, orphaned, but we have a father.

The first point to know about sonship is that the relationship is ordained by God. You don't go seeking a spiritual father. Look at the example of Esther, her parents died. She didn't go trying to find a spiritual father. God connected Esther to Mordecai because he was connected to her destiny.

My point is a spiritual father and child are always connected in God's purpose and destiny. If you feel as though you need a spiritual father don't go seeking one God will send you the right people at the right time. Let's study on.

It was Mordecai who introduced Esther to her assignment on the earth to be a queen.

Esther 2:10-11 (NKJV)

10 Esther had not revealed her people or family, for Mordecai had charged her not to reveal it.

11 And every day Mordecai paced in front of the court of the women's quarters, to learn of Esther's welfare and what was happening to her.

Esther didn't reveal her nationality because her spiritual father told her not to. My point the responsibility of a spiritual son (gender neutral) is to be obedient. They must be obedient to God and their spiritual fathers.

Even when out of Mordecai's presence Esther behaved herself as a woman of character and dignity. Spiritual fathers always give wise counsel. What we do when we leave their presence is up to us.

Again, the responsibility of a spiritual son is to be obedient. The responsibility of a spiritual father is to give wise counsel, to disciple.

Note in verse 11 Mordecai was acting as the father that he was and was being a protective father. Imagine you are a daughter or you have a daughter, they go on a date, but you spend the entire time at the door waiting for them to go home.

Again, fathers protect. Mordecai was a protective father. Some may have even thought of Mordecai as an overprotective father, but I like Mordecai. He was doing the right thing.

Spiritual sons and daughters when your spiritual parents are trying to protect you, don't rebel against it accept it. This is what love does. Mordecai didn't drop her off at the king's palace when she was 18 and was on his way. No, he showed genuine concern for her. Mordecai would not let up. He stayed at that gate. You got to love Mordecai what an awesome father.

Esther 2:19-23 (NKJV)

19 When virgins were gathered together a second time, Mordecai sat within the king's gate.

20 Now Esther had not revealed her family and her people, just as Mordecai had charged her, for Esther obeyed the command of Mordecai as when she was brought up by him.

21 In those days, while Mordecai sat within the king's gate, two of the king's eunuchs, Bigthan and Teresh, doorkeepers, became furious and sought to lay hands on King Ahasuerus.

22 So the matter became known to Mordecai, who told Queen Esther, and Esther informed the king in Mordecai's name.

23 And when an inquiry was made into the matter, it was confirmed, and both were hanged on a gallows; and it was written in the book of the chronicles in the presence of the king.

Notice Esther continued to obey Mordecai command after she was in the position. Look at verse Mordecai goes back sits at the king's gate in concern for Esther. Esther still is obedient. A son that is disobedient is rebellious and a dishonor to God and their parents.

To make a long story short, Mordecai discovers a plot to kill the people of Israel. This is exactly why obedience is so important. Had Esther revealed her ethnicity she would have been killed. I'll let you read the story for yourself. To make a long story short, Mordecai has to push Esther into her destiny.

Remember a good spiritual father always pushes you into purpose. They are not content for you to be comfortable. When it was time to step up, Esther was a little nervous, but she was willing to step into her rightful position within the kingdom even if it cost her, her life.

Spiritual fathers know when to let you lead. Spiritual sons know when to step up with the support of their father. Let's go back to the conversation between Mordecai and Esther.

Esther 4:10-17 Living Bible (TLB)

10 Esther told Hathach to go back and say to Mordecai,

11 "All the world knows that anyone, whether man or woman, who goes into the king's inner court without his summons is doomed to die unless the king holds out his gold scepter; and the king has not called for me to come to him in more than a month."

12 So Hathach gave Esther's message to Mordecai.

13 This was Mordecai's reply to Esther: "Do you think you will escape there in the palace when all other Jews are killed?

14 If you keep quiet at a time like this, God will deliver the Jews from some other source, but you and your relatives will die; what's more, who can say but that God has brought you into the palace (Kingdom) for just such a time as this?"

15 Then Esther sent this message to Mordecai: 1

16 "Go and gather together all the Jews of Shushan and fast for me; do not eat or drink for three days, night or day; and I and my maids will do the same; and then, though it is strictly

forbidden, I will go in to see the king; and if I perish, I perish."

17 So Mordecai did as Esther told him to.

Mordecai wasn't just an over protective father. If he was he wouldn't have pushed Esther to her purpose at the threat of her life. My point, here is the relationship between a true father and a true spiritual son (daughter).

Mordecai knew how to lead, Esther knew when it was time to step up and lead.

My point is Mordecai represents the relationship we have with God the Father and us. You may have a spiritual father, and that is great, but if you don't have a spiritual father, God Himself will still Father you. You have a responsibility to obey, to have a relationship, to know when it is time to step out on God's command.

Esther could walk in divine confidence because of her love for God and because she had a father. No, he wasn't her birth father. She didn't have a mother, but she had someone so much better.

When you are a true son or daughter of the highest God, you have a responsibility to walk worthy of who your Father has told you, you are, to obey at all cost, and to walk in divine favor and integrity.

By the way, I said a woman can't be a spiritual father and I meant it. A man can't be a spiritual mother. These are two distinct roles that God ordained within His kingdom. We live in a day where men are stripped from being men, and women are stripped from being women. That old spirit of Jezebel back at it again.

Nevertheless, if you want examples of a spiritual mother, the story of Ruth, Naomi, and Prophetess Deborah is great examples.

We can't talk about the responsibility of true sonship without talking about perverted sonship.

If there is one thing, I believe has robbed many believers of their positions of authority it is the perverted father relationship and perverted sonship. We have to get healed from it, so I have to expose it for healing to take place. Keep reading our next chapter is about perverted sonship.

Chapter 10

Perverted Sonship

1 Samuel 15:23 (KJV)

23 For rebellion is as the sin of witchcraft, and stubbornness is as iniquity and idolatry. Because thou hast rejected the word of the Lord, he hath also rejected thee from being king.

We must talk about what perverted sonship is. Before we go on there, we must ponder the question about motivation. What motivates you? What drives you to succeed? I have found that often we can have impure motives for wanting success. Perverted sonship is when we seek people, father figures, people in positions of prominence and authority to fulfill a desire for validation. This in part was one of Jezebel's problems, although she had some other issues that we won't have time to go into.

Validation is recognition or affirmation that a person or their feelings or opinions are valid or worthwhile. We must seek validation from God and God alone. Many want positions of leadership because they secretly want validation. They want the world at their feet, oohing and awing at them.

My pastor told us the other day, if you are going to be a leader you have to be okay with not being liked, you have to be okay with people talking about you. Being a leader requires tough skin.

Ironically most people want the prominence of leadership they don't want the cross that leadership bares. Let 's talk about perverted sonship. I am going to have you read some scripture before I go into the meat of what we need to hear. This is a very interesting story. To give the backdrop, David is getting ready to die. He is very old, and he needs to give final instructions of what will take place after he dies. David had a lot of children, which came with a lot of drama. I will spare you the details because it is not important to our current text. Yet, it is important to note if you want to study in detail perverted sonship, look at the life of some of David's children.

For the sake of this chapter, we are going to highlight, David's son Adonijah. I know the text it quite long, but I promise it is very interested and an easy read. Adonijah knows that David is getting ready to die. He decides he wants to be king, and well you must read the text.

1 Kings 1:1 (TLB)

1 In his old age King David was confined to his bed; but no matter how many blankets were heaped upon him, he was always cold

1 Kings 1:5-53 Living Bible (TLB)

5 At about that time, David's son[a] Adonijah (his mother was Haggith) decided to crown himself king in place of his aged father. So he hired chariots and drivers and recruited fifty men to run down the streets before him as royal footmen.

6 Now his father, King David, had never disciplined him at any time—not so much as by a single scolding! He was a very handsome man and was Absalom's younger brother.

7 He took General Joab and Abiathar the priest into his confidence, and they agreed to help him become king.

8 But among those who remained loyal to King David and refused to endorse Adonijah were the priests Zadok and Benaiah, the prophet Nathan, Shimei, Rei, and David's army chiefs.

9 Adonijah went to En-rogel where he sacrificed sheep, oxen, and fat young goats at the Serpent's Stone. Then he summoned all of his brothers—the other sons of King David—and all the royal officials of Judah, requesting that they come to his coronation.

10 But he didn't invite Nathan the prophet, Benaiah, the loyal army officers, or his brother Solomon.

11 Then Nathan the prophet went to Bathsheba, Solomon's mother, and asked her, "Do you realize that Haggith's son, Adonijah, is now the king and that our lord David doesn't even know about it?

12 If you want to save your own life and the life of your son Solomon—do exactly as I say!

13 Go at once to King David and ask him, 'My lord, didn't you promise me that my son Solomon would be the next king and would sit upon your throne? Then why is Adonijah reigning?'

14 And while you are still talking with him, I'll come and confirm everything you've said."

15 So Bathsheba went into the king's bedroom. He was an old, old man now, and Abishag was caring for him.

16 Bathsheba bowed low before him.

"What do you want?" he asked her.

17 She replied, "My lord, you vowed to me by the Lord your God that my son Solomon would be the next king and would sit upon your throne.

18 But instead, Adonijah is the new king, and you don't even know about it.

19 He has celebrated his coronation by sacrificing oxen, fat goats, and many sheep and has invited all your sons and Abiathar the priest and General Joab. But he didn't invite Solomon.

20 And now, my lord the king, all Israel is waiting for your decision as to whether Adonijah is the one you have chosen to succeed you.

21 If you don't act, my son Solomon and I will be arrested and executed as criminals as soon as you are dead."

22-23 While she was speaking, the king's aides told him, "Nathan the prophet is here to see you."

Nathan came in and bowed low before the king,

24 and asked, "My lord, have you appointed Adonijah to be the next king? Is he the one you have selected to sit upon your throne?

25 Today he celebrated his coronation by sacrificing oxen, fat goats, and many sheep, and has invited your sons to attend the festivities. He also invited General Joab and Abiathar the priest; and they are feasting and drinking with him and shouting, 'Long live King Adonijah!'

26 But Zadok the priest and Benaiah and Solomon and I weren't invited.

27 Has this been done with your knowledge? For you haven't said a word as to which of your sons you have chosen to be the next king."

28 "Call Bathsheba," David said. So she came back in and stood before the king.

29 And the king vowed, "As the Lord lives who has rescued me from every danger,

30 I decree that your son Solomon shall be the next king and shall sit upon my throne, just as I swore to you before by the Lord God of Israel."

31 Then Bathsheba bowed low before him[b] again and exclaimed, "Oh, thank you, sir. May my lord the king live forever!"

32 "Call Zadok the priest," the king ordered, "and Nathan the prophet, and Benaiah."

When they arrived,

33 he said to them, "Take Solomon and my officers to Gihon. Solomon is to ride on my personal mule,

34 and Zadok the priest and Nathan the prophet are to anoint him there as king of Israel. Then blow the trumpets and shout, 'Long live King Solomon!'

35 When you bring him back here, place him upon my throne as the new king; for I have appointed him king of Israel and Judah."

36 "Amen! Praise God!" replied Benaiah, and added,

37 "May the Lord be with Solomon as he has been with you, and may God make Solomon's reign even greater than yours!"

38 So Zadok the priest, Nathan the prophet, Benaiah, and David's bodyguard took Solomon to Gihon, riding on King David's own mule.

39 At Gihon, Zadok took a flask of sacred oil from the Tabernacle and poured it over Solomon; and the trumpets were blown and all the people shouted, "Long live King Solomon!"

40 Then they all returned with him to Jerusalem, making a joyous and noisy celebration all along the way.

41 Adonijah and his guests heard the commotion and shouting just as they were finishing their banquet.

"What's going on?" Joab demanded. "Why is the city in such an uproar?"

42 And while he was still speaking, Jonathan, the son of Abiathar the priest, rushed in.

"Come in," Adonijah said to him, "for you are a good man; you must have good news."

43 "Our lord King David has declared Solomon as king!" Jonathan shouted.

44-45 "The king sent him to Gihon with Zadok the priest and Nathan the prophet and Benaiah, protected by the king's own bodyguard; and he rode on the king's own mule. And Zadok and Nathan have anointed him as the new king! They have just returned, and the whole city is celebrating and rejoicing. That's what all the noise is.

46-47 Solomon is sitting on the throne, and all the people are congratulating King David, saying, 'May God bless you even more through Solomon than he has blessed you personally! May God make Solomon's reign even greater than yours!' And the king is lying in bed, acknowledging their blessings.

48 He is saying, 'Blessed be the Lord God of Israel who has selected one of my sons to sit upon my throne while I am still alive to see it.'"

49-50 Then Adonijah and his guests jumped up from the banquet table and fled in panic; for they were fearful for their lives. Adonijah rushed into the Tabernacle and caught hold of the horns of the sacred altar.

51 When word reached Solomon that Adonijah was claiming sanctuary in the Tabernacle, and pleading for clemency, 52 Solomon replied, "If he behaves himself, he will not be harmed; but if he does not, he shall die."

53 So King Solomon summoned him, and they brought him down from the altar. He came to bow low before the king; and then Solomon curtly dismissed him.

"Go on home," he said.

Adonijah, although he was the blood son of David, was a perverted son. The first thing we must know about Adonijah is how he got there. If you go back to verse 6, it said, "David never disciplined him."

Adonijah was a spoiled brat who was entitled. His father didn't discipline him or check him as a child, so he grew up as an undisciplined adult. He wanted a position that he was not qualified to handle.

The first point about perverted sons is that they, cannot handle being disciplined. We already talked about how God disciplines us in love. As son of God, we don't have to like being disciplined, but we do have a responsibility to submit to it.

The next thing we know is Adonijah a perverted son was that he was motivated by self. According to verse 5, he decided to crown himself as a king. A perverted son gains influence by promoting themselves. Modern day examples are individuals who can't submit to their leader, when their leaders don't promote them into positions of authority they leave the church and start their ministries. There is nothing wrong with leaving a church to start your ministry if that is what God has told you to do. God knows the heart. You have to make sure your motives are pure. Hopefully, you have the blessing of your leaders.

Adonijah was wrong, and he knew he was wrong. How do I know this because David had some key appointed leaders? Verse 8, some of the leaders were Priest Zadok, Prophet Nathan, Shimei, Rie and David's commander and chief. They wouldn't sign off on Adonijah's plans. So Adonijah got his own leaders who had titles to sign off on his crooked plot. My point is just because someone has other leaders attached to their influence or their platform doesn't mean they have been endorsed by God.

Perverted sons have influence, but they have not been promoted by God, they have been promoted by themselves and by people. In today's language you know perverted sons because they are always on social media promoting themselves, their product, their seminars, they may say something about God, but most of it is about self-promotion. They have no desire to promote or advance the kingdom of God.

You know modern day perverted son because they are always posting on social media about who does and doesn't like them. They are always talking about haters and jealous individuals. I was participating in a seminar years ago, and the founder was a minister. In the back of her table, she had rows of t-shirts that she was selling, all the shirts had hater this and hater that quotes. Can you say insecure? Walking around with a t-shirt that promotes your haters is a sure sign that you are insecure.

Nevertheless true sons are promoting the kingdom. In fact, when Solomon is put into position as king, He still seeks God for wisdom and understanding. His heart was right, look at God's response to Solomon.

1 Kings 3:6-12 (NKJV)

6 And Solomon said: "You have shown great mercy to Your servant David my father, because he walked before You in truth, in righteousness, and in uprightness of heart with You;

You have continued this great kindness for him, and You have given him a son to sit on his throne, as it is this day.

7 Now, O Lord my God, You have made Your servant king instead of my father David, but I am a little child; I do not know how to go out or come in.

8 And Your servant is in the midst of Your people whom You have chosen, a great people, too numerous to be numbered or counted.

9 Therefore give to Your servant an understanding heart to judge Your people, that I may discern between good and evil. For who is able to judge this great people of Yours?"

10 The speech pleased the Lord, that Solomon had asked this thing.

11 Then God said to him: "Because you have asked this thing, and have not asked long life for yourself, nor have asked riches for yourself, nor have asked the life of your enemies, but have asked for yourself understanding to discern justice,

12 behold, I have done according to your words; see, I have given you a wise and understanding heart, so that there has not been anyone like you before you, nor shall any like you arise after you.

Do you see the difference? True sons seek to advance the kingdom of God first. Perverted sons only seek to promote the kingdom of God after their plans have not worked. Perverted sons seek wealth, prominence and positions. They seek the things first.

True sons seek to advance God's kingdom.

Matthew 6:33 (KJV)

33 But seek ye first the kingdom of God, and his righteousness; and all these things shall be added unto you.

Other things that Adonijah did was to promote himself. He gave himself a coronation service. A coronation is a ceremony of crowning a sovereign or a sovereign's consort, similar to what we do in the US called the inauguration day. Adonijah promoted himself to the public to gain followers. Nevertheless, David promoted his son Solomon behind closed doors and then exposed him to the public to confirm what was done in private. We know this because David had long declared that Solomon would be king many years before he promoted him as king. That is why Solomon was one of the people not invited to the coronation service of his brother Adonijah.

Wow! I just said something power; it is worth repeating. Saint's when God is going to appoint you He will always do it in private, but He will expose you in public when He has finished preparing you for the position. Perverted sons will publicly promote themselves, while they have no integrity, no character, and no wisdom that is required for the position. They haven't allowed God to promote them behind closed doors. They couldn't submit to the process.

There is so much more I can say, I gave you a lot of scripture, but you get the point. So how does this relate to divine confidence? I am glad you asked.

This is what the Lord told me, "often we gain a false sense of confidence from the exposure." Meaning we get false confidence from people, from the accolades and from the position. That is not the will of God. If you get confidence from people the minute they don't like you, your confidence is gone.

You must check your motives. Perverted sons are insecure, proud and they don't have the heart for God. They follow God with their mouths, but their hearts are far from him. Solomon started out with a spirit of humility, and God honored him.

Maybe if David had disciplined Adonijah, he would have turned out better. If you read the story of Adonijah, he was still trying to plot to be king even after David had died. Unfortunately, being a perverted son ran in the family. Adonijah's big brother was Absalom; he did the same thing. You would think that Adonijah would have a clue of what not to do.

David was considered one most prominent and well-known kings that Israel ever had. His children were dysfunctional and a mess. On a side note for ministers, don't be the greatest minister to others to the neglect of your children and wife. Or vice versus women in ministry, don't be a world success and neglect your husband and children. Chaos broke loose in David's home, but he had a clear pattern of not disciplining his kids when they did wrong.

What motivates you? Sometimes you think you have pure motives, but you don't. God knows the heart. I have had times where I was driven to accomplish things, and God had to correct me and put me back on course.

Let your confidence be in God. Let your motives be to advance His kingdom. Commit to being a true son. Trust me

God wants true sons. This generation is missing it, but as stated there is a group, a remnant which God is going to move through in great and mighty ways. Their hope and their heart are first in Jesus.

Chapter 11

When Father's Kill

1 Samuel 19:2 (NKJV)

2 So Jonathan told David, saying, "My father Saul seeks to kill you. Therefore please be on your guard until morning, and stay in a secret place and hide.

We have painted a pretty picture when it comes to fathers, but the reality is for us to be healed and set free, we must get free from the rejection wounds of a father. We talked a lot of David's and his son. Let's go back to the beginning. What happens when the love of the father goes cold? What if the father you loved, turns his affection to hate, and then he tries to kill you? Maybe he assassinates your character; maybe he tries to stop your progress. How do you forgive? And believe it or not, if you are going to be a success you are going to have to forgive.

Let's go back to the beginning of David's life. We touched on this some in an earlier chapter but as stated we will need to revisit this in more detail for healing to take place. When you read David's beginnings, he was rejected by his biological father. Saul was king at the time, but God fired Saul because of his repeated rebellion and disobedience against the word of the Lord. So, God told the Prophet Samuel that Saul is fired and he was to anoint another a king.

This leads us to our first point rebellion; disobedience will always lead you outside of the will of God. Then God says to the Prophet,

1 Samuel 16:1 (NKJV)

16 Now the Lord said to Samuel, "How long will you mourn for Saul, seeing I have rejected him from reigning over Israel? Fill your horn with oil, and go; I am sending you to Jesse the Bethlehemite. For I have provided Myself a king among his sons.

We know that David is rejected because when the prophet arrives at his father Jessie's house, they all gather with excitement over a lavish meal. David was never invited to the feast. In fact, Prophet Samuel had asked was someone missing, because David's father forgot to mention the fact that he had a son outside in the field tending sheep.

David position outside was an indication of his rejection. He was an outsider to in his own family. He was not invited in, but God had a plan.

Did you know that your promise will cause you to be rejected? David is anointed in front of his brothers, and the hatred and resentment that his brothers had towards him intensifies. David was not close with his biological brothers. You read the initial dynamics between Saul and David.

Remember we said that David and Saul were once close. Saul was a spiritual father, David was his spiritual son.

1 Samuel 16:16-21 (TLB)

15-16 Some of Saul's aides suggested a cure.

"We'll find a good harpist to play for you whenever the tormenting spirit is bothering you," they said. "The harp music will quiet you and you'll soon be well again."

17 "All right," Saul said. "Find me a harpist."

18 One of them said he knew a young fellow in Bethlehem, the son of a man named Jesse, who was not only a talented harp player, but was handsome, brave, and strong, and had good, solid judgment. "What's more," he added, "the Lord is with him."

19 So Saul sent messengers to Jesse, asking that he send his son David the shepherd.

20 Jesse responded by sending not only David but a young goat and a donkey carrying a load of food and wine.

21 **From the instant he saw David, Saul admired and loved him; and David became his bodyguard.**

How do you go from loving someone to trying to kill them? Imagine the pain the David goes through he is finally excepted; his loved tank is filled, and then in an instant, he is running for his life. That is enough to make a person bitter, angry and resentful. When you read the life of David, he handled himself well. He never sought revenge; he didn't try to explain himself.

His trust was in God, and because his trust was in God when he was betrayed he drew closer to God. David didn't have the best parenting skills, but he loved God. Hurt, betrayal, rejection, disappointment should always lead you closer to God. Nevertheless, often times if a person allows it will lead them away from God. The question remains what happened? Many of you know the story of David but humor me for a minute we must get free from what lies beneath. It is the invisible seed that the enemy plants in our subconscious, if we don't check it, and deal with it, it will destroy relationships.

Remember I said Saul was like a spiritual father to David, any real father that is secure wants their son to be better and greater than them.

1 Samuel 18:6-14 Living Bible (TLB)

6 But something had happened when the victorious Israeli army was returning home after David had killed Goliath. Women came out from all the towns along the way to celebrate and to **cheer for King Saul,** and were singing and dancing for joy with tambourines and cymbals.

7 However, this was their song: "Saul has slain his thousands, and David his ten thousands!"

8 Of course Saul was very angry. "What's this?" he said to himself. "They credit David with ten thousands and me with only thousands. **Next they'll be making him their king!"**

9 So from that time on **King Saul kept a jealous** watch on David.

10 The very next day, in fact, a tormenting spirit from God overwhelmed Saul, and he began to rave like a madman. David began to soothe him by playing the harp, as he did

whenever this happened. But Saul, who was fiddling with his spear,

11-12 suddenly hurled it at David, intending to pin him to the wall. But David jumped aside and escaped. This happened another time, too, for Saul was afraid of him and jealous because the Lord had left him and was now with David.

13 Finally Saul banned him from his presence and demoted him to the rank of captain. But the controversy put David more than ever in the public eye.

14 David continued to succeed in everything he undertook, for the Lord was with him.

I am going to say something, and I don't want you to take it lightly. I have witnessed this to the depth of my soul. I have cried many tears not understanding this one principle. I had to forgive based upon what I am about to tell you, even when it hurt.

The truth is everyone cannot handle your success. Saul knew at some point God was no longer with him, and that God would replace him. Remember in an earlier chapter we talked about the Pharaoh who plotted against Moses and then again Jesus. Well, it was the same spirit operating in Saul. Notice there was a celebration in Saul's honor, but they ended up celebrating David. Well, they should have, David had just killed Goliath. The truth is David hadn't killed ten thousand people yet, but the honor was due to him at that time because he did have a great battle and rightfully, so they should have celebrated him. It may have been rude for them to compare Saul to David at Saul's party. Think about that it, that is like going to a birthday party for a friend, and they spend the entire time talking about how your other friend's birthday party that happened last weekend was much better.

The truth is people will be people. Sometimes people can be offensive intentionally and unintentionally. Whatever the reason, this incident angered Saul. Saul should have dealt with the people who were being rude at his party instead of taking it out of David. I think he knew secretly after the celebration that David was his replacement. David didn't do anything wrong. He won a battle, loved God and loved Saul.

I know we all want to hate on Saul right now, but I want us to see things from Saul's eyes just for a minute.

Saul was the king of Israel. Saul had prestige and a position of prominence. This no named boy comes along, and it appears he has not accomplished nowhere near what Saul has accomplished at that time and all of the sudden people put David above Saul. Again, this is David pre-reign of being king; he was just starting out, don't think of David as the dynasty that he became, think of him as a boy just starting out. No name, no reputation, no nothing and overnight he was being compared to a king. I am not justifying Saul's actions, but if we be honest we can see it from Saul's perspective. We don't have to agree with it, but we can see it. I am going somewhere hang in there, okay I know I am giving you a lot of information.

Sometimes God will reveal things in you, that you don't know are there. Let me tell you about me. I am a woman who has accomplished a lot, by the grace of God. A while back I had an incident where I had completed a major project. I had partnered with another entrepreneur. As it turns out, they were extremely busy, and I ended up doing most everything including using my own money to complete the project. They were very unreliable and to be honest, not professional. Because my name and reputation was attached to the project I just spearheaded it because I didn't want to take the hit if it didn't work out. It turns out the project ended extremely well. This is where it got concerning for me and God had to check me.

At the end of our working project, people were in awe of what was done. Even though I did everything, everyone that saw our project was giving this person praises and telling them how much of a wonderful job they did. Even though behind the scenes they did nothing but show up, to present. Hopefully, you are seeing how is going? I noticed it instantly, but I am not a petty betty, so I didn't say anything about it. I didn't correct the people. I didn't say such and such did nothing. I just knew at the end of the day; I couldn't work with them again. Not because I didn't get praise but because I honestly know that I cannot partner with someone who can't help or bring anything to the table.

It took a lot of time, work, money, and effort to complete the project. My next idea moving forward is if I am going to partner with someone I need people who can pull their weight.

I had to be honest with myself, even though I shrugged it off, I kept thinking about it, underneath my positive attitude it bothered me a bit. There are times when God uses situations to teach me lessons about myself; sometimes they are for my next writing project, sometimes they are for both. Whatever the reason they are always opportunities for my personal growth.

I talked to God about it. God told me that in my subconscious mind, He allowed this incident to break something in me. You see secretly I wanted validation and praise from people. I didn't get it. The lesson for me was to break me from the opinions of people. This is a lesson that I have had many times. I thought I passed that test, but every now and again you need a refresher course. Then God spoke to me about me. I had to clutch my pearls. Me God? Well God knows the hidden agenda of my heart. I would never think of myself as an envious of someone. I am not jealous. Jealous is when you want what someone else has. I don't want anything anyone else has. God didn't tell me I was jealous.

God did tell me I had a competitive spirit. A spirit of competition is as good as or better than others of a comparable nature. I want to be the best. I don't compare myself to anyone, but I always know that I win in every circumstance. Sounds positive right. Well no in many cases it was not. Although I am not jealous or envious of anyone, when this person was given the accolades that I felt belonged to me, it invoked an envious spirit. Why? Because I felt my partner was given accolades and praise for something that should have been given to me.

I had to repent and check that at the cross. Yes, it is true I did do everything, I have the receipts to prove it. Yes, it is true that my partner just showed up when it was convenient. What was not appropriate was how I felt.

God was using this to help me. You see every spiritual parent wants to see their children to better than they have. Sonship becomes perverted when the father comes jealous of the son because the son did just what the father prepared him to do. This is when sonship gets perverted.

Therefore, we have to submit our need for validation to the foot of the cross. There is no need for a spirit of competition within the body of Christ. No, I will not partner with this entrepreneur because I truly needed help, help that they couldn't provide. Nevertheless, I also must know who I am and whose I am. There are different assignments I have within my purpose. One of those assignments that I don't talk about often is that I am a leader amongst leaders. I have the mandate to teach and train others who are called into positions of leadership. I can't be envious when they do what I have trained them to do. God was using this incident as my training ground.

Let me give you another example. We see this very often in church when an individual is mentored by a church leader; sometimes it is an individual disciple, other times it can be a teacher from afar. God opens the door for the individual and the same leader that mentored them then tries to destroy their character and kill their God-given assignment.

Whenever someone is trying to kill your purpose, they are acting as a spiritual Saul. The reason why I brought this up is that I don't want to be a Saul to others and neither do you. Therefore, we must correct our motives. Our confidence must be built on Christ alone. Saul messed up a great relationship. Yes, David was his replacement but had he treated David right, David would have honored Saul until his death. Saul ended up committing suicide. We must humble ourselves and let go of pride.

Proverbs 16:18 (KJV)

18 Pride goeth before destruction, and a haughty spirit before a fall.

Haughty means arrogantly superior and disdainful. Synonyms include proud, arrogant, vain, conceited, snobbish, superior, self-important, pompous, supercilious, condescending.

Had Saul's heart been correct he would have prepared David, by mentoring him for his reign. Some of you think that is crazy for him to do but remember what we said about true spiritual fathers. Look at what Jesus did to prepared us as His spiritual sons.

John 14:12-14 King James Version (KJV)

12 Verily, verily, I say unto you, He that believeth on me, the works that I do shall he do also; and greater works than these shall he do; because I go unto my Father.

13 And whatsoever ye shall ask in my name, that will I do, that the Father may be glorified in the Son.

14 If ye shall ask any thing in my name, I will do it.

Jesus taught so we could lead, then He says, "you are going to do greater things than me."

Luke 10:1 (NKJV)

10 After these things the Lord appointed seventy others also,[a] and **sent them** two by two before His face into every city and place **where He Himself was about to go.**

Minus David's lacking good parenting skills, for the most part, we all want to be like David. Yet, where there are spiritual David's you would have to have overcome a spiritual Saul.

What about David's response? David responded with wisdom regardless of the attacks against him. David had the opportunity to kill Saul, but he didn't. In fact, this is so good we have to read this together.

1 Samuel 23:28 New King James Version (NKJV)

28 Therefore Saul returned from pursuing David, and went against the Philistines; so they called that place the Rock of Escape.[a]

Saul was determined to kill David, so he was actively pursuing him.

1 Samuel 24 Living Bible (TLB)

24 After Saul's return from his battle with the Philistines, he was told that David had gone into the wilderness of Engedi;

2 so he took three thousand special troops and went to search for him among the rocks and wild goats of the desert.

3 At the place where the road passes some sheepfolds, Saul went into a cave to go to the bathroom, but as it happened, David and his men were hiding in the cave!

4 "Now's your time!" David's men whispered to him. "Today is the day the Lord was talking about when he said, 'I will certainly put Saul into your power, to do with as you wish'!" Then David crept forward and quietly slit off the bottom of Saul's robe!

5 But then his conscience began bothering him.

6 "I shouldn't have done it," he said to his men. "It is a serious sin to attack God's chosen king in any way."

7-8 These words of David persuaded his men not to kill Saul.

After Saul had left the cave and gone on his way, David came out and shouted after him, "My lord the king!" And when Saul looked around, David bowed low before him.

9-10 Then he shouted to Saul, "Why do you listen to the people who say I am trying to harm you? This very day you have seen it isn't true. For the Lord placed you at my mercy back there in the cave, and some of my men told me to kill you, but I spared you. For I said, 'I will never harm him—he is the Lord's chosen king.'

11 See what I have in my hand? It is the hem of your robe! I cut it off, but I didn't kill you! Doesn't this convince you that I am not trying to harm you and that I have not sinned against you, even though you have been hunting for my life?

12 "The Lord will decide between us. Perhaps he will kill you for what you are trying to do to me, but I will never harm you.

13 As that old proverb says, 'Wicked is as wicked does,' but despite your wickedness, I'll not touch you.

14 And who is the king of Israel trying to catch, anyway? Should he spend his time chasing one who is as worthless as a dead dog or a flea?

15 May the Lord judge as to which of us is right and punish whichever one of us is guilty. He is my lawyer and defender, and he will rescue me from your power!"

16 Saul called back, **"Is it really you, my son David**?" Then he began to cry.

17 And he said to David, "You are a better man than I am, for you have repaid me good for evil.

18 Yes, you have been wonderfully kind to me today, for when the Lord delivered me into your hand, you didn't kill me.

19 Who else in all the world would let his enemy get away when he had him in his power? May the Lord reward you well for the kindness you have shown me today

20 And now I realize that you are surely going to be king, and Israel shall be yours to rule.

21 Oh, swear to me by the Lord that when that happens you will not kill my family and destroy my line of descendants!"

22 So David promised, and Saul went home, but David and his men went back to their cave.

When I read this passage of scripture I cried. David honored Saul even when most of us wouldn't. When you read on Saul didn't keep his word. He had a change of heart and ended up trying to kill David repeatedly. Each time David responded with integrity.

I could go on, but this is a true example of when sonship is perverted because the father goes awry. I want to talk to someone who has been hurt, betrayed by someone they loved. Maybe it was a spiritual father; maybe it was a pastor, maybe it was a friend. I am on the verge of tears because I have been a spiritual David, to my knowledge God checked me before I ever became a spiritual Saul. Nevertheless, as stated the potential is there if we don't obey the warning of the father. First, you must forgive. Don't let what it has done to you rob you of your peace. What happened to David could have made him bitter, angry, resentful, wrathful, and revengeful.

In fact, let us look at another one of my Facebook posts;

Beloved one when people have an issue with you, and you have only treated them with kindness and respect, don't take it to heart. The truth is they are secretly intimated by your success, so their minds create problems that don't exist. This is called projection they project their insecurities on to others instead of owning it and bringing it to the cross.

Your response is to forgive and move on. Why spend head space about someone who is not attached to your purpose, destiny or assignment. Somethings are not worth worrying about. My advice don't keep thinking about, posting about, or talking about it. LET IT GO! Your anointing is valuable; your destiny is secure, why lose your peace over what doesn't matter?

People that are not for you DON'T matter. Focus on the ones that are.

Yes, I have some enemies, some haters, some jealous folks who don't understand what it cost me. I have learned people become resentful because they see your success and assume it came easy while they are struggling. All the while they have no idea the struggle you went through behind closed doors. But you know what I am so focused on where God is taking me they are a non-factor in my life.

Don't try to justify how or why you are successful.

Value your peace and do what is necessary to keep it.

You must let it go. Without forgiveness you allow the plot of the enemy to bring low confidence and low self-esteem on to you. You begin to question yourself, your worth. Particularly when you have been rejected by people you love. I have learned and had the hurt of betrayal all because God placed his hand on my life. I have people who don't want to hang out with me anymore, don't want to return my phone calls, never check to see if I am alive and I didn't do anything. I have had my closest friend try to destroy my reputation, my career, and my very soul. Yes, honestly at the time it brought me low. I kept thinking what did I do to them? The truth is I did nothing.

David did nothing wrong. The truth of the matter is Saul was trying to sabotage the plan of God. Had David not had a forgiving heart, Saul's plans would have succeeded.

If you have experienced anything like this, you must forgive. Let it go. Don't let the spiritual father's betrayal cause you to miss your destiny. It hurts but you know what? In the long run, it helps.

So how does this relate to confidence? It is simple, being rejected by someone you love hurts. You start second-guessing yourself. You start doubting yourself. You even start doubting what God has called you to. How?

Because being validated by people gives you a false sense of security. If you don't learn who you are, you gain confidence from people and the minute they don't like you then your identity is gone. Think about the celebrity who falls from grace or lose their money, and they think "now who am I." Think about the mother who lost herself so much in her kids by the time they move on as young adults; the mother has no identity because it was wrapped into being someone else. Think about the marriage that ends in an affair; now someone is left devastated and questioning their identity. My point is not to bring you low. The truth is people will change their minds, one minute they will put you on a pedestal and the next minute they will take you off. Change is inevitable, and no matter how much it hurts people have the right to change their minds. The ones that once loved you will betray you.

When I this happened to me I was devastated, I was hurt, the emotional pain cut like a knife.

In fact look at what David said;

Psalm 55:12-14 Amplified Bible, Classic Edition (AMPC)

12 For it is not an enemy who reproaches and taunts me—then I might bear it; nor is it one who has hated me who insolently vaunts himself against me—then I might hide from him.

13 But it was you, a man my equal, my companion and my familiar friend.

14 We had sweet fellowship together and used to walk to the house of God in company.

It is the ones closes to you, the ones you shouted with, the ones you attended church with that betray. David had many enemies; we learned later that his children were his enemies.

His children tried to kill him. His spiritual father tried to assassinate him on multiple occasions.

This could potentially devastate a person's soul. Therefore, our trust and validation must come from God. The truth of the matter is no matter how holy and Christian you are there is a Saul on the inside of you that you must bring under subjection. There is a part of you that wants to deal with your enemies. Confidence in God gives you hope after betrayal and lets you know that God is your source.

When these events happened, I questioned a lot of things in my life. Still, because it happened at a time that I matured in God, I never questioned who I was in Him. I knew that it was a part of His plan. I also learned that this person could not join me in my future. You see there are some people that cannot handle where God is taking you, but out of loyalty and love, we keep them around knowing that it is not God's will to bring them into destiny with us.

Beloved, we must look to our brother David, forgive and lean closer to God. To close this chapter let's get some final words of encouragement from or brother King David.

Psalm 27 Living Bible (TLB)

1 The Lord is my light and my salvation; he protects me from danger—whom shall I fear?

2 When evil men come to destroy me, they will stumble and fall!

3 Yes, though a mighty army marches against me, my heart shall know no fear! I am confident that God will save me.

4 The one thing I want from God, the thing I seek most of all, is the privilege of meditating in his Temple, living in his presence every day of my life, delighting in his incomparable perfections and glory.

5 There I'll be when troubles come. He will hide me. He will set me on a high rock

6 out of reach of all my enemies. Then I will bring him sacrifices and sing his praises with much joy.

7 Listen to my pleading, Lord! Be merciful and send the help I need.

8 My heart has heard you say, "Come and talk with me, O my people." And my heart responds, "Lord, I am coming."

9 Oh, do not hide yourself when I am trying to find you. Do not angrily reject your servant. You have been my help in all my trials before; don't leave me now. Don't forsake me, O God of my salvation.

10 For if my father and mother should abandon me, you would welcome and comfort me.

11 Tell me what to do, O Lord, and make it plain because I am surrounded by waiting enemies.

12 Don't let them get me, Lord! Don't let me fall into their hands! For they accuse me of things I never did, and all the while are plotting cruelty.

13 I am expecting the Lord to rescue me again, so that once again I will see his goodness to me here in the land of the living.

14 Don't be impatient. Wait for the Lord, and he will come and save you! Be brave, stouthearted, and courageous. Yes, wait and he will help you

Thank you David, you were not the best parent, who am I to judge, but you made an excellent king. Thank you for those words of encouragement.

Chapter 12

Divine Confidence

Joshua 1:9 (KJV)

9 Have not I commanded thee? Be strong and of a good courage; be not afraid, neither be thou dismayed: for the Lord thy God is with thee whithersoever thou goest.

We are just about at our end. My least favorite thing about writing a book is getting to the end believe it or not. I want to tell you so much more. I want to tell you that you do have it in you and that regardless of what it looks like right now God is going transform you in such a way you won't recognize yourself. There is so much more, but any good minister must know when it is time to end. Beloved, we must end our journey here. I want to leave with some final tips on how to walk in confidence from God.

I was at a meeting with a group of ladies about two weeks ago, and we were talking about how to cultivate a relationship with God. I said, "you have to be intentional about your relationship with God." One of the ladies asked, "what do you mean by that?"

I responded it is like any relationship. If you have a spouse, but you never spend time with them, even though technically on paper you have a relationship, you may even see each other daily, but you have no relationship. In any relationship you must spend time talking to one another, getting to know one another, and growing together. Many marriages end because each one says, "they grew apart." That is an indication that they intentionally didn't do things that would intentionally have them to grow together. Intimacy is not always sex; it means closeness, oneness, and willingness to be completely vulnerable and exposed.

It is the same way with God. There are some people who on paper are Christian, but the only time they hear from God is when they go to church on Sunday and have their preacher speak a word from God. After Sunday morning service is over, they go home, sit God back in a corner and never think, or speak to Him again. Some people only call on God when they are in a crisis. If you only have a relationship with God for two hours on Sunday, you have no relationship. What if you only saw your spouse for two hours a week, how long would you be married? What if you only saw your spouse when you were in a crisis how would you feel? Again, how long would you stay married? Would you meet a potential mate and only call them during a crisis? Would you have been married at all? Something to think about.

We treat God worse than we treat any human being but expect blessings and power to be released into our lives. My point is if we are going to walk in diving confidence we must be intentional about our relationship with God. Confidence is released through a relationship with God first. The more you grow in Him, the more confident you become.

Other tips to get to divine confidence in God.

Joshua 1:8 (KJV)

8 This book of the law shall not depart out of thy mouth; but thou shalt meditate therein day and night, that thou mayest observe to do according to all that is written therein: for then thou shalt make thy way prosperous, and then thou shalt have success.

Psalm 1:2 (KJV)

2 But his delight is in the law of the Lord; and in his law doth he meditates day and night.

Scripture meditating is not the same as what the world does. Meditating is not sitting on the floor with your knees crossed, your hands in the air and your eye closed. That is called foolish. Scripture calls this vain repetition. This is how they teach you to meditate in the secular world. Vain repetitions mean the action of repeating words that have no meaning.

Meditating in Christ is the intentional and repetitive act of thinking upon the word of God and reciting the word of God. We are not meditating for meditating sake; we are meditating or reciting the word. Meditating is not a religious act or regimen; it is establishing a relationship with God.

All meditating is taking a scripture or scriptures and implanting them into yourself, so your soul will begin to mend.

You must be careful what you think on.

Have you ever had a favorite song you loved so much that you kept it on repeat? This past week I have been listening to a song sung by Miranda Curtis, Let Praises Rise. I have worn that song out it has been on repeat. Guess what I was doing? Meditating.

Another example, I went to church yesterday, the word of God was amazing. I listened to the same word after church it was so good. Then on my hour-long commute to get to my office today, I listened to the same message the entire way. What was I doing? Meditating. What was I meditating on? The word of God. I was not meditating on my pastor or his style of preaching; I was repeatedly listening to the word of God, he was the vessel being used.

You do have to intentionally read the word of yourself. Still, there are additional ways to meditate on the word. This is, so the word of God gets in your system. As stated worship songs, inspirational messages, doing what you are doing today, reading. You start with reading the Bible and then progress in other ways to meditate on the word of God throughout your day. This morning I got up for my prayer time with God, and I studied my word. My point is listening, and hearing from others is not a replacement for your own time spent with God, in your alone time with Him. As much as I want you to read my books, as much as I know that they are scripturally sound, if all you do is read books like this and never spend time with God, reading scripture on your own, you are doomed to fail.

You must be careful what you feed your spirit. If you listen to a bunch of hip-hop music that is full of obscenities and vulgarity, you will take on that spirit and not the Holy Spirit. The Holy Spirit will not listen to obscenities and vulgarity so when you allow that in your spirit on a consistent basis, the Holy Spirit is a gentleman he will leave because you are showing him he is not welcome. Remember at the beginning divine confidence comes from the word of God.

I don't watch or listen to anything that is not edifying to my spirit. People may call me deep, but you must know what you must do to stay in God-confidence and in your right mind.

Colossians 3:16 (KJV)

16 Let the word of Christ dwell in you richly in all wisdom; teaching and admonishing one another in psalms and hymns and spiritual songs, singing with grace in your hearts to the Lord.

The word of God is powerful. The word of God is not repeating vain words. The more you digest the word of God, the stronger you become.

Hebrews 4:12 (KJV)

12 For the word of God is quick, and powerful, and sharper than any twoedged sword, piercing even to the dividing asunder of soul and spirit, and of the joints and marrow, and is a discerner of the thoughts and intents of the heart.

When we meditate on the Word of God, it begins to transform us, because the word is not ordinary. The word is not vain words. The word of God has supernatural power. The more you get in your system it becomes healing power, it begins to break off fear, doubt, low confidence and anything else that has attached itself to our hearts that don't belong.

We must also be diligent about what we allow our thoughts to ruminate on. Ruminate means to think deeply about something. Ruminate is to go over in mind repeatedly and often casually or slowly; to chew repeatedly for an extended period. Ruminate is another word for vain repetitions. In the previous chapter, we talked about forgiveness. If you keep replaying in your mind what someone did to you and what happened, you haven't forgiven, and you are meditating on the wrong things. We must get rid of stinking thinking.

2 Corinthians 10:3-7 (NKJV)

3 For though we walk in the flesh, we do not war according to the flesh.

4 For the weapons of our warfare are not carnal but mighty in God for pulling down strongholds,

5 casting down arguments and every high thing that exalts itself against the knowledge of God, bringing every thought into captivity to the obedience of Christ,

6 and being ready to punish all disobedience when your obedience is fulfilled.

Caste means to throw away violently. Your thoughts can be your biggest bully. You must intentionally not allow your thoughts to run wild. Thoughts create feelings.

Proverbs 23:7 (KJV)

7 For as he thinketh in his heart, so is he: Eat and drink, saith he to thee; but his heart is not with thee.

You have to intentionally think positive on a consistent basis.

Philippians 4:8 (KJV)

8 Finally, brethren, whatsoever things are true, whatsoever things are honest, whatsoever things are just, whatsoever things are pure, whatsoever things are lovely, whatsoever things are of good report; if there be any virtue, and if there be any praise, think on these things.

In my counseling sessions, I have a worksheet, called attacking fear, that has turned into a workbook called, Fight Fear With Faith. In this worksheet I have them take a specific thought that they have been negatively ruminating on. We answer the following question.

Is this thought true? Yes or No. What makes it true? Can I think differently about it? Is this thought just (fair), lovely? Does this thought make me feel good or bad? Why doesn't it make me feel good or bad? How can I rethink this thought to fit scripture? Can I use this thought as praise? Yes or no? Why not? In what ways can you praise yourself? In what ways can you praise God? Ex: "I thank you of God that I am fearfully and wonderfully made.

Sometimes it is a matter of retraining your brain and have it submit to the will and the plans of God. God's plan for us is always good.

Jeremiah 29:11-12 King James Version (KJV)

11 For I know the thoughts that I think toward you, saith the Lord, thoughts of peace, and not of evil, to give you an expected end.

12 Then shall ye call upon me, and ye shall go and pray unto me, and I will hearken unto you.

God gave the people of Israel this declaration during a seventy-year sentence in captivity. God doesn't wait until your circumstance is right to declare His promises over your life. He gives you the promise either right before the storm or while you are amid the storm. It is our choice whether the plans that God has for us come to manifestation. We can decide we don't want God's plan. You may think no one would ever say they don't want the plan of God for their life. Still, when you choose to live a defeated life, you choose not to fulfill God's plan for your life.

Lastly to reiterate my point you must have faith. Faith doesn't come from thin or air. Faith doesn't come by osmosis. Osmosis is the process of gradual or unconscious assimilation of ideas, knowledge, etc. Faith come by hearing and hearing, and hearing the word of God. The more you hear the word of God, the more your faith begins to increase. The more faith you have, the more confident, you will be.

Romans 10:17 (KJV)

17 So then faith cometh by hearing, and hearing by the word of God.

You must hear the word of God. That means to get into a good church that teaches the word of God. I am not against whooping and hollering but shouting with no word is like eating a lot of processed food. You may get full temporary but in the end you end of feeling empty and still hungry. Go to a good word church. A word church is a church that puts emphasis on teaching the word of God. The pastor goes line by line teaching you the word. In my church, we love to praise God, but the word is what matters most. At my church, you must bring a notebook and take notes. This is what good students do, great leaders teach.

You know a word church by the depth of the teaching. There is nothing wrong with the gifts of the spirit but a church that puts more emphasis on the gifts of the spirit then the word of God is out of order to believe it or not. No, I am not against the gifts of the spirit. Though, if you look at the example of Jesus when He was on earth, he healed the sick, prophesied, and performed other miracles, but the most important thing He did more than anything else was to teach the word of God. That is why you have people calling Him teacher or Rabbi. Rabbi is another word for a Jewish teacher.

Miracles don't mature you. We read earlier how the people of Israel saw great signs, wonders and miracles, yet they still doubted God, and many didn't make it to the promise. Miracles don't indicate a relationship with God.

In fact, I was talking with a friend of mine the other day. She had recently joined a church and quickly started serving in ministry. Nevertheless, shortly after joining, she said her and her husband might be looking for another church. The reason being is because her husband felt like he wasn't getting anything out of the word. He felt as though he wasn't being fed. I just encouraged them to keep looking, but the truth of the matter is I agreed. Of course, I didn't say that to her.

They had invited me to the church briefly. I agreed to come and support, although I already have a great church, there is nothing wrong with visiting to support a friend. Well, the pastor's prophesied repeatedly, even prophesied over me accurately. Yet, there was no word, no real depth, no teaching just prophesying what God was getting ready to do, but no real solid word. I visited at least three times, and it was the same thing. Even if I were looking for a church home, I would join that church, and I do mean never.

My prophetic anointing is accurate. I am not bragging, but I can prophesy to myself. I can prophesy a generic prophetic word to myself. Yes, the prophetic is needed, but people's prophetic doesn't impress me. If you can teach the word of God, that is what impresses me. I love to learn. I love coming away feeling and knowing I have learned something I didn't know before.

Let me tell you a secret if you are anointed to pastor or lead, and you want to grow your ministry, learn how to teach. People are hungry for the word of God. Most people are over the entertainment, the shouting over a promise they want the word. If I get the word in me, I'll shout and prophesy over myself on my own time. When I go to church I want to be taught, not tantalized to shout.

My point is if you are at a church where your spirit is not being fed, find another church. You are not rebellious or ungrateful; you are caring for your inner man. I have been a member of a church where I was not being fed. I stayed there out of loyalty, and we were taught that it was sinful to leave a church. It is not sinful to leave a church if you are leaving with the right motives.

The church I go to now fills my love tank. Although my journey to confidence is from God alone. The single most important factor that led me to supernatural confidence was when God planted me in the right church. I had been on my journey long before I started attending my church, but it feels like when I finally got to the church I attend it catapulted me into levels of God-confidence that I had never experienced. That God confidence catapulted me into supernatural success in every area of my life. Remember the anointing flows through your God-confidence.

We are at our close. I pray that you have been blessed. My prayer is that you and many other believers would stand up a mighty confident army for the Lord. The world needs Christ, and we must be bold witnesses for Him.

Philippians 1:6 (KJV)

6 Being confident of this very thing, that he which hath begun a good work in you will perform it until the day of Jesus Christ:

Philippians 1:6 Living Bible (TLB)

6 And I am sure that God who began the good work within you will keep right on helping you grow in his grace until his task within you is finally finished on that day when Jesus Christ returns.

Be blessed and know God is rooting for you, so am I. In Him you will succeed.

Love

Samaria

About The Author:

Samaria was saved at eight years old. Shortly after that she received the baptism of the Holy Ghost. Samaria first received her call to ministry many years ago when attended to Bennett College in Greensboro, NC. After attending a youth-led Bible study, she learned that some things only come through fasting and prayer. The Lord impressed upon her to seek His face for what she needed to hear from Him. It was then that Samaria began to seek God for her purpose and destiny within the body of Christ. So after much prayer and fasting, God spoke to Samaria in a series of dreams and visions over a three year period. It was during this time that she experienced some of the greatest spiritual awakenings of her life. Her confidence in her relationship with God and His destiny for her life was certain.

Samaria Colbert is an anointed writer, licensed therapist, minister and consultant. She received her Bachelor's degree from Bowie State University, in Bowie, MD. She later went on to receive her Master's from Howard University, in Washington, D.C. She is currently pursuing a Ph.D. Samaria calls North Carolina home.

Samaria also has a heart to counsel; she is the founder and CEO of Kingdom Creative Counseling Services. The counseling part of her private practice is specifically for women, men, and children who have survived early childhood sexual abuse and domestic violence. Samaria uses an integrative approach to therapy that includes, mental health, inner healing, and deliverance, all biblically based so that complete healing and wholeness is achieved through Christ Jesus.

Samaria is also the founder and CEO of LIKEAPRO Professional Writing Services. An organization dedicated to a spirit of excellence and completing the writing projects for Christian professionals, lay persons, and fivefold ministers.

Samaria uses her skills and passion as a writer, teacher to develop informational training materials and conduct workshops on how to effectively use integrative therapy techniques in counseling practice.

She believes in, "Absolute abandonment for the cost of the call of Jesus Christ." Samaria is a young woman, who loves God, loves His word, and is passionate above all about His purpose and destiny for her life.

Stay tuned, the future looks bright, and there is so much more to come from this dynamic, anointed and appointed a woman of God.

"What will you do in your lifetime that will have an impact on someone else's life for a lifetime?"

Samaria M. Colbert

To stay up to date with her latest writing projects, ministry and to request her to speak at your event please visit her website.

www.samariacolbert.com

www.likeaprowritingservices.com

www.kingdomcreativecounseling.com

KCC

Kingdom Creative Counseling Services

MENDING BROKEN PIECES

Insurance accepted:

www.kingdomcreativecounseling.com

336-543-0159

Depression · Christ-Centered

Anxiety · Psychotic Disorders

Recovery from Early Child Sexual Abuse/Trauma

Domestic Violence · Recovery from Spiritual Abuse · Inner Healing and Deliverance

Play Therapy

Adults, Families, and Children Served

www.samariacolbert.com

www.likeaprowritingservices.com

LikeAPro Professional Writing Services

Make sure you pick up your very own copy of Samaria's other books:

No Promise Without A Process The Makings Of A True Prophet

The Wisdom To Fulfilling Your Prophetic Destiny. A Memoir of Words, Warnings, And Pitfalls To Avoid Missing Your Prophetic Destiny.

This I know: Because There Are Choices You Make That Can Either Birth or Abort Your Spiritual Destiny

God Can Change Anyone

No Promise Without A Process The Makings Of A True Prophet Part II

Inside Out Because Real Transformations Happens From The Inside Out Not The Outside In

To Whom It May Concern

Wisdom, Warnings and Warfare

Hearing The Voice of God

Demons, Deliverance and Spiritual Warfare

Soul Ties

Not Without A Struggle

Trusting God Is Not Easy But It Is Worth It

Not Without A Purpose

Deliverance From Depression

No More Fear

You Are Not Forgotten

The Process of Emotional Healing

The Process of Emotional Healing Workbook

The Process of Emotional Healing Facilitators Guide

A Ready Made Writer

Hidden To Lead

Healing The Heart Through Forgiveness

The Ministry of Honor

Broken

Kingdom Mandates, Kingdom Mantles and Kingdom Authority

The Heart Of Worship

Restoration

Psychological Warfare

The Wait

The Wait Individual Workbook

The Wait Facilitators Guide

The Wait 60 Day Devotional

Let Down Your Nets

The Bible And Business

Who Beguiled You?

According To Your Faith

Couches and Conversations Workbook Journal

Couches and Conversations Group Manual

Couches and Conversations book

Fight Fear With Faith Workbook

Training Manual
COUCHES
AND
CONVERSATIONS

COUCHES
AND
CONVERSATIONS

Samaria M Colbert

Couches and Conversations
TRAININGS COMING IN 2018

God the Father wants His children healed, whole, set free and delivered from all emotional wounds. Inner healing is a counseling ministry that God has ordained for Christian counselors, therapists, and ministers. Inner Healing is NOT the same as traditional mental health counseling. The author has a mandate from heaven to train Christian leaders to do the work of counseling ministry. This series includes the book;

- Couches and Conversations (Teaches Basic Inner Healing principles)
- Couches and Conversations (Journal Workbook)
- Couches and Conversations (For small group)
- Couches and Conversations (Teaches Inner Healing Implementation, and Methodology)

Coming in 2018 Training and Seminars for (Christian Therapist, Clinicians and Counseling Ministers).

CONTACT US IF YOU ARE INTERESTED IN SCHEDULING A TRAINING AND PRICING. VISIT THE CONTACT TAB

BOOKS AND TRAINING MATERIAL AVAILABLE DEC 1, 2017 VISIT THE BOOKSTORE TO PURCHASE. ALSO AVAILABLE ON AMAZON AND KINDLE

Kingdom Institute For Training Christian Professionals

K.I.T.C.P

For more information contact us visit the website at:

www.samariacolbert.com

www.samariacolbert.com

www.samariacolbert.com

www.likeaprowritingservices.com

www.samariacolbert.com

www.kingdomcreativecounseling.com

www.likeaprowritingservices.com

Made in the USA
Middletown, DE
27 September 2022